MW01068189

THE GOD DESIGN

Secrets of the Mind, Body and Soul

KELLY-MARIE KERR

With special contributions by author
JOHN R. FRANCIS

UKCS Registration Number: 284727419

www.seekvision.co.uk

ISBN 978-1-9164137-1-9

First Printing, 2019
Printed in the United Kingdom

DISCLAIMER:
This book contains general medical information only. NOTHING in this book is intended to be a substitute for qualified, certified professional medical or psychological advice, diagnosis or treatment. You must NOT rely on the information in this book as an alternative to medical advice given by a professional healthcare provider or doctor. Consult a qualified professional healthcare provider or Medical Doctor (MD) with questions or concerns regarding practices or substances mentioned in this book that may affect your health or general wellbeing. You should always seek immediate professional medical attention if you think you are suffering from any medical condition. The medical information within this book is provided without any representations or warranties, express or implied. The medical information contained within this book is not professional medical advice and should not be treated as such. The medical information contained within this book is ONLY provided to highlight comparisons within the topics presented here, further personal research and professional guidance is always recommended.

THE GOD DESIGN
Secrets of the Mind, Body and Soul

Acknowledgements

First and foremost, I am thankful to God, our Divine Creator for the blessing of life and all that it entails.

Special thanks to author John R. Francis PhD for his significant contributions to this book: writing the foreword, chapter 32, two insightful appendices and for proofreading the entire book. Thank you to God for the divine appointment you created in order to bring us together. John's time, enthusiasm and knowledge is greatly appreciated on all levels.

Special thanks to my generous supporters on Patreon who have made the fruition of this book possible: Cindy Jewell, Troy Skog, TJ Fingulin, Rachel Kate Munroe, Curtis Hewitt and Raymond Smith.

I would also like to thank my YouTube subscribers and Instagram, Facebook communities for their support, questions and encouraging comments. Also, to everyone who has visited my website and purchased a transcript or brought a T-Shirt – Thank you, the proceeds have really helped to "keep the light on".

Special thanks to my friend Lindsey Hunter who is a Kundalini instructor and the founder of "Lindsey Hunter Healing". She has read and approved of all the information within this book that relates to Kundalini.

Special thanks to my family and friends. Especially my wonderful husband and best friend Simon Gunn, my adorable baby boy Zackary and my peace-emanating fluffy side-kick-cat Simba. Also, my soul brothers: Darren Baba, Joe Deering and Christen Kwame, my soul sisters: Katherine Evans and Sally Whyte.

Last but by no means least, I would like to thank John St Julien, who is undeniably inspired by the love of God. His work in Tanzania is truly miraculous and I fully encourage both the financial and prayerful support of his charity "Share Tanzania".

Contents

Foreword
by John R Francis

You are now invited to read about the awakening and discovery of an ordinary woman named Kelly-Marie Kerr. Kelly-Marie is happily married and has a radiant, young son. She has enjoyed a career as an actress and screenwriter. Furthermore, she has directed her God-given gifts for communication into writing for her popular YouTube channel and a well-received "Freedom Yoga" iOS and Android App. But perhaps her most significant spiritual offering to date is the book you are about to read.

In this book, Kelly-Marie Kerr reveals the details of her spiritual awakening and subsequent discovery of a secret that has been hidden from the general public for thousands of years. The unearthing of these hidden teachings may be one of the keys that opens humanity to unimaginable possibilities and ushers in a new age of peace, love and true abundance on Earth.

My first contact with Kelly-Marie, just a few, short months ago, was no accident. I discovered her via the Internet by intentionally searching for those who had experienced a similar awakening to my own and were now part of a growing number of way-showers guiding humanity during this tumultuous time of transition. Each one of these beacons of light underwent a similar transformation during their awakening and each one has a unique gift and perspective to contribute to the collective consciousness expansive. Kelly-Marie is no exception.

Inner guidance informed me that as an "elder" my mission now is to seek out those who will be the torchbearers of the coming age of Light and Love. In doing so, I am to offer my assistance and encouragement to these spiritual leaders of the future. I then contacted Kelly-Marie, apparently at the perfect time. She had essentially completed the writing of this book and needed someone to do final proofreading. I welcomed the opportunity to volunteer my services.

After communicating with her, glancing through her manuscript and other resources on her website I quickly recognized that she has a unique and important mission and many gifts to share. I also discerned that she had a genuine spiritual experience and has pure motives in wanting to share her thoughts and insights.

I myself had a very profound awakening in 1975 and subsequently underwent major transformations. I intuitively knew that Kelly-Marie had also had an authentic spiritual opening based on my own inner awakening. During my experience, I was given a mission to decode the hidden teachings in the Bible that would be critical for the birth of a new human during the coming planetary "Apocalypse." This Greek word "apocalypse" means a revelation or an unveiling and not necessarily a cataclysmic ending. I remembered a prophecy in the Bible that says that "at the end of the age all that is hidden would be revealed" – both the positive and the negative.

As I looked at the manuscript of the book you are about to read, I recognized that Kelly-Marie had decoded many more Bible secrets in the short time since her awakening than I had uncovered during the past 44 years of my research. Perhaps this is explained by the acceleration of the speed of the planetary transformation in recent years and on the enhanced capacities of the new souls who are now coming into spiritual maturity and leadership on this planet now.

Nonetheless, I did feel I still had certain unique insights to offer to her book and mission. Much to her credit, she has been very open to what I had to share and accepted that which resonated with the intention of this current book.

My own studies revolve around decoding the parables of Jesus to reveal his secret teachings to his disciples. What I had previously found directly supported the discoveries of Kelly-Marie during her awakening and subsequent research. My discovery of the Spiritual Heart is that it has an intelligence that is deeper than the rational brain's intellect. Over the years, many hours of daily meditation have revealed an inner way for allowing the deep Love and Light of our being to shine through into our body and into the world in general.

I am honoured that Kelly-Marie has requested that I include a summary of my Spiritual Heart research and meditation in the appendix at the end of this book.

Before concluding this Foreword, I would like to share my insights into why the insights that Kelly-Marie is sharing in this book are so important at this critical junction in our planetary evolution.

Since the Industrial Revolution, human technological development has been increasing exponentially. Consequentially, there have been radical alterations of the natural world in the industrialized areas of the planet. Some would argue that these changes have not all been improvements - air, water, food and electromagnetic pollution, crime, poverty and the looming threat of nuclear war. Technology has been sold to the masses as the way to improve the human condition without much attention being given to the obvious, unintended negative consequences.

The technological revolution is not just being directed to the external environment but also to the human body itself. A new field called transhumanism is emerging that promises a radical enhancement of the human body through genetic manipulation and the merging of human and machine. There are predictions of great increases in longevity and even the achievement of human immortality in the near future.

Based on the history of technological development, one would be justified to ask if there will also be serious, unintended negative consequences to the attempts to modify the human body through genetic-bioengineering and computer interfacing.

One widely accepted scientific model says that humans are nothing but mechanical machines. What we call consciousness is nothing but the activities of neurons in the brain. It is suggested that there is no consciousness independent of the human brain; no soul or Spirit. Further claims allude to the idea that there is no God or spiritual intelligence guiding human evolution and thus there is no higher purpose to life in this matter model.

This book proposes a very different view of what it means to be a human and the inner potential we all have that can be activated and realized. The vision it presents for humanity is based upon a marriage of forgotten ancient-spiritual wisdom encoded in the Bible and the latest scientific research of credentialed and courageous leading-edge scientists.

Unfortunately, most theologians today only see the literal level of the Bible. They fail to recognize the metaphors and symbols that convey deeper meanings to "those with eyes to see and ears to hear" (Matthew 13:16). Consequently, their interpretations "miss the mark" by seeing the Word of God primarily as a book of prophecies and moral precepts.

In "THE GOD DESIGN: Secrets of the Mind, Body and Soul", Biblical symbols and metaphors will be decoded with the aid of mystical insights and the corroboration of the latest scientific discoveries and theories. What will be revealed is the marvellous design of the human body – "made in the image and likeness of God" (Genesis 1:27). However, this spiritual design awaits our consent and cooperation to be nurtured and ignited.

We may well be living in the prophesied "end of an age" (Matthew 28:20 KJV) when all secrets will be revealed (Luke 8:17 KJV). Therefore, we must be "doers of the Word and not just hearers" (James 1:22 KJV).

Street-corner prophets shout that Jesus is coming soon. They say all we need to do is believe and in the twinkling of an eye we will all be magically transformed. No knowledge or inner discipline is needed according to them.

Thus, it is no wonder that materialistic science rules the day and spirituality and religion are belittled. The Bible is too often seen as a book of contradictions and childish stories meant to be the "opiate of the masses."

It is to the science of mainstream biology and computer engineering that so-called "sophisticated" people today look to provide a utopia on earth where, according to them, humans and machines could merge to create a glorious "transhuman."

However, this book questions this vision and instead reveals a hidden design that God has created in each of us. The glorious biology within that can give birth to a new "resurrected" human – "Christ within, the hope of glory". This can fulfil the prayer: "Thy Will be done on Earth as it is in Heaven." (Matthew 6:10 KJV).

This book systematically reveals the God Design within us in a way that is very accessible and requires no scientific training or deep metaphysical experience to understand. It is also very practically oriented, emphasising inner experience and discipline over intellectual gymnastics.

The science presented in this book is not intended to be a substitute for faith. Honest, truth-seeking science bolsters faith in God. The understanding that true science brings can strengthen our belief in a God Who is always within us and has created us with a higher purpose in Mind.

Throughout this book our inner, sacred anatomy is revealed. This is done by combining allegorical insights into Biblical mysteries with the latest discoveries in science. In particular the discoveries and theories linking biochemistry and states of consciousness are most helpful. Furthermore, extensive references are given so the reader can do independent research to verify the conclusions offered in this book.

Specifically, this book discusses the scientific discovery of biochemicals, naturally produced in the human body, and associated neurophysiological structures that facilitate the awareness of realms of existence beyond ordinary, physical reality. Serious, credentialed scientists are cited in this book, who based on careful experimentation, have concluded that these experiences in altered states of consciousness are as real as our physical reality. They are not mere hallucinations of the brain. This of course contradicts the mainstream scientific belief that the physical world is all that exists. However, these contradictory, new scientific research findings are consistent with the experiences that mystics have been reporting for thousands of years – from all spiritual and religious traditions and parts of the world. Certainly, the Holy Bible contains numerous such accounts.

However, even though the human body contains naturally occurring biochemicals that can induce altered states of awareness, this book is definitely NOT advocating the ingestion or any other means of intaking the same or similar chemicals that may be found in nature or synthesized in the laboratory for various reasons. First of all, if they are illegal then we would never want to encourage violating a governmental law. Secondly, it is very important that a person be prepared through the proper discipline and inner purification of body, mind and soul before the activation of the body's inner design for experiencing expanded states of awareness.

Actually, even though this book gives a detailed description of the inner process of biochemical transformation, this book is NOT advocating that such activation be the primary focus of one's spiritual practices. Rather this book advocates inner purification and the love of God and neighbour as the focus. If that is done, then when the disciple is ready the inner activation will occur spontaneously and safely.

There are some who advocate bypassing those commandments and speeding the process by the intake of psychoactive substances. The temptation often is for instant, psychic powers or information that can be used to create technologies that will make one wealthy, powerful and famous. If one's motives are impure then when taking those substances contact will be made with deceptive, psychic beings during the psychoactive, psychedelic experience who are equally impure. Like attracts like in the psychic realm. The desired psychic powers and information can be obtained but the consequences will prove to be detrimental for the individual experiencer and all of humanity.

This book offers insights for a life filled with love, clarity and confidence for those who seek "the straight and narrow path to God." The reader will find a balance of theory and practice in this book. You will also find that ancient, spiritual wisdom is confirmed by the latest scientific discoveries and interpretations. Finally, links are provided to research resources that complement and supplement this book. The reader is particularly encouraged to take advantage of the expert materials and services of the author of this book, Kelly-Marie Kerr. Her website is www.seekvision.co.uk

CHAPTER 1

Seek Ye First

"But seek ye first the kingdom of God, and his righteousness; and all these things shall be added unto you."

Matthew 6:33 (KJV)

On the 7ᵗʰ of July (7-7) I unwittingly woke up 7 times during the night and recorded 7 dreams which I found scrawled in my journal the next morning:

7 DREAMS
1. An empty YouTube channel with the title: "Seek Vision"
2. Talking to a man who revealed himself to be Jeremiah
3. My beloved primary school teacher playing "Seek Ye First" on the piano
4. News reports about the "Brussels calamity"
5. A lush hotel room brimming with cakes, chocolates and champagne and me being violently disgusted by it

6. My father-in-law telling me that I will become a "passionate and creative evangelist"
7. A huge pair of hands in the sky, a small pair of hands on earth and a tiny pair of hands below them.

At this time, I did not know as much about numerology and gematria as I do now, but I did know that the number seven was significant Spiritually and Biblically. The first and third dreams immediately made me think of Matthew 6:33; a scripture that has always been prominent in my life. Instinctively I always knew that this verse encapsulated something profound, but I never quite managed to find the time or focus to figure out the deeper meaning and exactly how amazing the divinity within this promise was, until, that is, I put the instruction into action and literally began to "Seek God first".

My "Seeking" lead to the gradual but complete abandonment of all negative influences including; unhealthy relationships, over use of social media, drinking alcohol and other body-abusing, time-devouring distractions. In favour of these low vibration habits I increased my Bible study, prayer time and meditation. My yoga practise evolved from what I simply used to call, "prayer yoga" to becoming an entire compilation of every yogic element taught by the primitive Christians known as the Essenes. The culmination of these focuses made me start to notice "synchronicities" happening all around me, my dreams became clearer and more poignant and an intense healing took place in me; mind, body and spirit.

During this time, I had an incredible dream where I could see a rainbow of colours inside my body, each colour was corresponding with a beam of energy entering my body; my gaze followed the beams of colour into the heavens where they shone with such vibrance that the light caused me to awaken. Reflection and study of these images lead me to a deeper understanding of the 7 candlesticks in the book of Revelation and the 7 chakras/energy centres of the body.

"SEEKING"

Sometime later whilst reflecting upon notes that I had made in my journal, I rediscovered the dream I'd had of a YouTube channel, "Seek Vision". "Seek Vision, Seek Vision" I repeated in my mind over and over again, "what does that REALLY mean?" I wondered. Soon I was studying the two words, both "seek" and "vision" independently and together.

"Seek" from the old English "Scan" means to: inquire, pursue, desire and EXPECT FROM. I learned that when it comes to God, "seeking" is a perpetual pursuing of God's presence, consequently I found out that, "presence" is a common translation for the word "face" and thought to myself "where will I find God's face…?" This train of thought reminded me of a powerful Bible scripture:

> "And Jacob called the name of the place Peniel:
> for I have seen God face-to-face, and my life is
> preserved"
>
> **Genesis 32:30 (KJV)**

Feeling a little confused, I returned to prayer and silent time, "Where will I find your face Lord?" I asked, "I thought your presence was EVERY-WHERE?" I continued. Suddenly and unexpectedly I heard God's voice; quietly, but distinctively say:

"I am here, I am always here, but there are periods when you forget to think of me. You take no time to seek guidance and neglect to put your trust in me; therefore, you find my glory "unmanifested". My "face", my light, my presence becomes hidden behind a veil of your desires. That is why you must "seek" continuously."

I realised through further meditation and Bible study that seasonal devotion and occasional doubt were creating the illusion of separation from God. "Carnal desires", meaning - animalistic urges such as greed, ego, lethargy and lust were distracting me from finding true contentment and purpose, thus creating "enmity against God" (Romans 8:7 KJV). I felt like God wasn't there or didn't care, because my "seeking" wasn't consistent.

My sudden, deeper understanding of this scripture made me feel like I had shed a layer of skin, I felt lighter and freer. I cried tears of joy at the thought of God's eternal presence and light sustaining and governing everything. It was as though the words were transforming my thoughts and perceptions as I truly began to know, not just "believe", but KNOW that God is eternally committed to loving us, uplifting us and aligning everything to work for our greatest good. It is only our carnal senses that trick us into feeling like God is not always with us. We all have times when we are busy and prioritize other things before God; forgetting to "seek" and becoming neglectful. It is during these times that our frustrations deepen, and God appears to have left us. God's shining face and the exuberance of unconditional love and power does indeed become hidden behind the veil of our carnal desires. This "(d)evil" is always there, ready to "kill, steal and destroy." JOHN 10:10

"VISION"

Of course, I then felt compelled to understand the word "vision" and have it resonating inside me in the same way as the word "seek", so I began to investigate:

VISION:

1. The faculty or state of being able to see
2. The ability to think or plan the future with imagination and wisdom
   - IMAGINATION: Creative POWER, intuition, FOREsight
   - WISDOM: Applied knowledge
3. "Something seen in the imagination or in the SUPERNATURAL"

I took this to mean that vision is much more than physical sight, but rather, it is "God's supernatural sight" and that is what I should be continually "seeking" or pursuing. I understood that if I did not "seek vision" then I was inadvertently allowing "reality" to create my life for me, and that living without vision; imagination or creative power I was passively susceptible to being "tossed to and fro" (Ephesians 4:14) and blown where ever the currents of life took me. I had to take authority, I had to centre my thoughts, emotions and actions to align them with God. Over the following days I repeated the question to myself over and over and over again; "who am I and what can I do for God?"

That night when I was trying to sleep the most incredible thing happened, I felt waves of heat rushing up my spine and my head felt like it had been enlarged a hundred times or more. I instantly sat up in elation, wondering what was happening, but not wanting it to end. A series of images flooded through my brain with such clarity that they looked and felt totally real. I saw blue oil flowing upward – defying gravity, a tiny seed of perfect life emanating the purest light, my tongue set ablaze by a roaring fire, a website entitled "Seek Vision" with the four creatures of Ezekiel stood behind the title and a black and white explainer video explaining the *true anointing of Christ*. Once the sensation had disappeared, I began to cry, and a feeling of intense love was filling me up;

mind, body and soul. There was a newness in me, my energy increased, my focus increased, I needed less sleep to function, it was like I'd had an injection of super powers.

The following days were a blur of excitement, I felt a childlike awe for EVERYTHING I saw and touched. The world was literally brighter; the colours were more vivid, and the atmosphere had an added dimension to it; I knew that I'd had "a moment", a "visitation" or "something" and although it was immensely powerful, I instinctively knew that a small piece of the puzzle was still missing. I was so moved by my experience that I wasn't sure whether to share it with anyone and everyone who would listen or keep it all to myself! I was looking into all possible inter-pretations available for my visions at all given moments; searching the Bible for "blue oil" and the internet for "light seeds" and "the anointing oil", but nothing seemed to relate to my journey or make obvious sense to me, until one day when I was sat reading emails and saw an update message from YouTube – I usually deleted these types of emails before even opening them, but with a little extra time on my hands I opened it to see a list of "recommended videos", one of which caught my attention: "Jim Carey Spoke on the Greatest Secret In Humanity" and so I, of course, followed the link. I found a man whom I'd never seen before but felt an instant humanly unexplainable platonic, spiritual attraction to – it was John St Julien, God bless him, talking about the "Sacred Secretion" and INSTANTLY I KNEW that this was what I had experienced and that the internal Christ Oil was indeed, *the true anointing of Christ.*

I was ecstatic and practically leapt for joy. I picked up my Bible and reread the story of Jacob and it felt as though the words were alive; I could see them vibrating inside me. Every passage that I read had new-living-meaning. It was simply the most incredible revelation of my life. After that I knew EXACTLY what to do, I needed to use my passion for writing, teamed with the knowledge of physiology and anatomy that I had learned through studying yoga and dance, fuelled by my love for God and the Bible to create an explainer video for the Sacred Secretion or *the true anointing of Christ*. Since publishing that initial video to YouTube I have received literally thousands of emails and comments asking me, "how do I raise the oil?", "when does the Sacred Secretion take place in the body?" and "What exactly is the Sacred Secretion?" all of which are questions that I have endeavoured to answer and explain as thoroughly and clearly as possible within this book.

CHAPTER 2

The Sacred Secretion

"Chemistry is the physical expression of Alchemy, and any true knowledge of chemistry is: not the knowing of the names of the extracts and essences, and the plants themselves, and that certain combinations produce certain results, obtained from blind experiments, yet, prompted by the Divine spirit within; but knowledge born from knowing the why and wherefore of such effects. WHAT IS CALLED THE OIL OF OLIVES IS NOT A SINGLE, SIMPLE SUBSTANCE, BUT IT IS MORE OR LESS COMBINED WITH OTHER ESSENTIAL ELEMENTS, AND WILL FUSE AND COALESCE WITH OTHER OILS AND ESSENCES OF SIMILAR NATURE. The true chemist will not limit his researches to the mere examination, analysis and experiments, in organic life; but will inform himself equally in physical astrology."

(Page 57) [Alchemy] "The Light of Egypt" by Thomas H Burgoyne

The name "Sacred Secretion" refers to the "substance" that anoints the body. As the quote states, the "Sacred Secretion" is not merely a "single, simple substance." Therefore, this analysis will endeavour to explain all aspects of it; not only the physical attributes of this "substance", but also the all-important metaphysical or Spiritual attributes of this "substance".

The Metaphysical meaning of the word substance is, "the spiritual essence out of which all things are made" (The Truth Unity Metaphysical Dictionary). It is visible to the mind through dwelling on the idea of "being", but our five physical senses cannot feel or appreciate it. Mostly, "substance" is not recognised because the world is focused on effect rather than cause; matter rather than essence.

Throughout history this substance has been known by many names and described in various exoteric and esoteric ways. Although no two understandings are identical, they each propose the same underlying facts. The teachings include, but are not limited to: Manna from Heaven, Merkabah, the Alchemical Wedding, Kundalini, Clavis Rei Primae, XXenogenesis, Naronia, the crystalline dew of the adepts, the Tibetan Rainbow body of Light and the Christian Resurrection Body. Due to the power of this phenomenon a lot of the information has been sequestered away and altered to appear in many different guises. Over time this has created the illusion of separate processes or practises that oppose one another in essence and form instead of bolstering each other and illustrating unity in their one common sacred, freedom-creating truth.

The hidden nature of the Sacred Secretion means that the recent discovery of it by a broader audience has provoked a lot of questions and misunderstandings. In order to reveal a comprehensive description of the process, including the spiritual and material interpretations of it, I have endeavoured to put the prominent puzzle pieces into place - that we may have a clearer and more holistic knowledge of this magnificent gift.

"There is an automatic procedure within the human body, which, if not interfered with will do away with all sickness, trouble, sorrow and death, as stated in the Bible."

Page 21, "God-Man: The Word Made Flesh" by George W Carey & Ines Eudora Perry

CHAPTER 3

The Secretion – Introduction

"But the anointing which ye have received of him <u>abideth in you</u>, and ye need not that any man teach you: but as <u>the same anointing teacheth you of all things</u>, and is truth, and is no lie, and even as it hath taught you, ye shall abide in him."

1 John 2:27 (KJV)

The mind and the body of man have the power to transform divine energy from God's etheric plane of unconditional love and limitless power to the earthly plane. This is the power and dominion that God planted in humans from the beginning.

The internal anointing or Sacred Secretion that "abideth" within us to be examined and explained throughout this book is a combination of two main elements:

1. THE SPIRITUAL PROPERTIES: The influx, preservation and transformation of spiritual "substance" (divine energy), which we are continuously receiving from God and of God.

2. THE PHYSICAL PROPERTIES: The internal biological upgrade of Melatonin into the powerful metabolites that all work simultaneously to produce the physical sensation associated with the preservation of the Sacred Secretion.

There is nothing in the human organism with more potential for magnificence or devastation than this intricately powerful force. Subsequent chapters will explain both the spiritual and biological components of the Sacred Secretion and how, like any living organism it can flourish or perish depending on how it is treated and what it is exposed to.

CHAPTER 4

The Secretion – Spiritual Properties

"The menorah and its utensils are to be made of
sixty-six pounds of pure gold. See that you make
them according to the design being shown you
on the mountain."

Exodus 25:39-40 (CJB)

The Menorah is an ancient symbol shaped like a tree or a candlestick with seven branches. It was known in antiquity as the, "Tree of Life" within the human body. Speaking to Moses on Mount Sinai (Exodus 25:31-40), God handed down specific instructions for how his Temple (a reflection of the human body) was to be built and for the Menorah, which was to be placed inside the temple. God said that the Menorah was to be made of hammered Gold and hold seven candles; three on each side, with a central stem. Interestingly, the word "Menorah" has been avoided in many translations of the Bible but is still present in original Hebrew translations and the Tree of Life Version (TLV). The seven candles relate to several different things, for example; seven major glands of the physical body, seven energy centres (Chakras) of the spiritual-subtle body and seven planetary influences, all of which are a reflection or correspondence to one another.

Simply stated Macrocosm, Microcosm means big universe, little universe. Among others, Plato recognised the clear parallels that can be drawn between the universe and the human organism. Robert Fludd's, "Images of the Divine" are a set of incredible engravings that show this divine correspondence with clarity and beauty. God created these wonderful layers of creation to miraculously complement and connect with one another and then told Moses to make an ornament, the Menorah, that signified this divine process: God's divine energy flowing through the seven prominent planets and into the seven energy centres (Chakras) of the body.

> "Speaking of the ancients: "They believed in a quite literal way that nothing inside us is without a correspondence in nature. Worms, for example, are the shape of intestines and worms process matter as intestines do. The Lungs that enable us to move freely through space with a bird-like freedom are the same shape as bird wings. The visible world is humanity turned inside out." "To the teachers of the mystery schools it was significant that if you looked down on to the internal organs of the body from the skies, their disposition reflected the solar system."
>
> (Page 54) "The Secret History of the World" by Jonathon Black.

There are many ways to perceive these layers of creation and there are certainly many more layers than will be discussed here; some paradigms put the human mind first, emanating the universe from the inside out, and some vice versa.

The adept will be familiar with a description far more complex than what I will describe here; starting with the "Solar Logos" and the "Monad" and incorporating the Solar angel, Atomic body, Buddha body, Casual Body, Lower mental body, Astral body, Etheric Body and the Condensed elemental (physical) body. But, for now, the four layers that God showed me and are detailed here will be a helpful foundation for learning:

LAYER ONE: GOD – Divine Energy - Created all things and is in all things.

LAYER TWO: SPACE - God created the planets and their energetic influences (seven of which are prominent and therefore integral to this study).

LAYER THREE: PHYSICAL HUMAN – God created us to have an outward experience of life that can be a lesson and testament to others, helping to evolve the collective consciousness.

LAYER FOUR: SPIRITUAL HUMAN – God created a reflection of the first 3 layers within us; including a spiritual energy centre (chakra) and nerve plexus correlating with each planet and, the "seed" which travels through the spinal cord or internal river Jordan mirroring the physical life of Christ.

Just as the Spiritual Substance of the Sacred Secretion from God, permeates to each of us through these four levels and ignites or anoints our being, the oil within the Menorah lamp anoints or ignites the seven flames of the tree.

"Thou anointest my head with oil; my cup runneth over."

Psalm 23:5 (KJV)

To summarise, the Spiritual composite of the Sacred Secretion is: The uniquely aspected divine energy that incorporates a cocktail of stellar and planetary influences that are specific to each of us individually during a particular time of the month. If the divine energy can flow freely through our chakras in an environment of love, peace and surrender without being "wasted", it will rise to the thalamus and enlightenment will occur.

These points, their relevance and how to calculate the timing of the Sacred Secretion will be referred to and explained in more depth throughout this book.

CHAPTER **5**

The Secretion – Physical Properties

The first chemical to be addressed when understanding the physical side of the Sacred Secretion equation is DMT. However, DMT is not the only chemical responsible for the heightened sense of consciousness achieved by preserving the Sacred Secretion.

Dimethyltryptamine (DMT)

More than just a natural plant hallucinogenic, Dimethyltryptamine (DMT) is the only known endogenous (self-produced) psychedelic within the human organism. Labelled the "Spirit Molecule", by Rick Strassman, DMT is prominently found in human Cerebral Spinal Fluid (CSF) and has the ability to harmonize our voltage-gated sodium channels (Na+ channels). Voltage-gated sodium channels play an important role in "action potentials". If enough channels open, a change occurs in the cell's membrane potential and a significant number of Na+ ions move into the cell via their electrochemical gradient and further shift electric charge distribution within the cell. In other words, DMT has the potential to assist the body's bioelectricity thus optimising cell health and activity.

"Moreover, DMT, the only known mammalian *N,N*-di-methylated trace amine, can activate the sigma-1 receptor to modulate Na+ channels."

Science. 2009 Feb 13; 323(5916): 934–937 "The Hallucinogen N,N-Dimethyltryptamine (DMT) Is an Endogenous Sigma-1 Receptor Regulator" by Molly Johannessen

DMT is a naturally occurring tryptamine derived from the amino acid Tryptophan, as are; Serotonin – produced by nerve cells and found in blood platelets throughout the central nervous system, and melatonin – the regulator of biological rhythms produced by the pineal gland. In fact, the difference between Melatonin and DMT is minute. The only difference in their molecular structures is one atom of carbon and two atoms of oxygen which is equal to just one molecule of carbon dioxide.

Simply stated:

MELATONIN – CARBON DIOXIDE (CO2) = DMT

Mildly reduced carbon dioxide levels elevate brain and lung pH levels (more on pH in chapter 33) causing pH dependent enzymes, such as INMT (Indolethylamine-n-methyltransferase) to encourage endogenous DMT formation. Since the relationship between carbon dioxide and melatonin allows for DMT to be produced it is important to look at how carbon dioxide levels in the blood peak and trough. Carbon dioxide levels are affected by a whole host of things; muscle activity, food metabolising, air quality and breathing patterns. For example, deep breathing such as is used in meditation gives the desired effect of decreasing carbon dioxide in the blood whereas overeating raises it.

DMT is also comprised of serotonin, melatonin and a cocktail of other psychedelic tryptamines such as 4-AcO-DMT, 5-MeO-DMT, 5-HO-DMT, psilocybin (4-PO-DMT), and psilocin (4-HO-DMT). The fact that this extremely potent psychedelic chemical flows through our cerebrospinal fluid accounts for many of the miraculous experiences that we enjoy and witness through living a conscientious life of love, peace, joy, gratitude and understanding but as previously stated it does not act alone.

In order to understand the Sacred Secretion and how to preserve it, we must understand the biosynthesis of DMT within the Pineal Gland. Tryptophan is vital in the human body's production of DMT. Figure 1. (below), taken from "Dark Retreat" by Mantak Chia shows a summary of the transmuting relationship between Tryptophan and DMT.

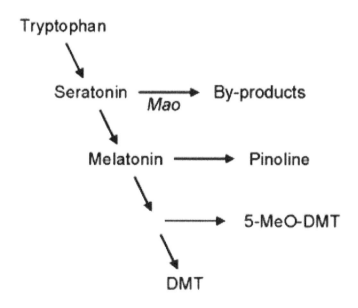

FIGURE 1. TRYPTOPHAN & DMT

Basically, what we are seeing here is the process of how tryptophan must first produce serotonin before serotonin can produce melatonin and ultimately melatonin can produce several other biochemicals responsible for the effects associated with the preservation of the Sacred Secretion. These biochemicals are: pinoline, mexamine, benzodiazepine, tryptoline and luciferin binding protein (LBP). Let's take a closer look at these fascinating chemicals one by one.

TRYPTOPHAN

Tryptophan is at the root of this transformational process. It is an essential amino acid available only from food (pumpkins, walnuts and oats are among the best vegan sources). Tryptophan assists with nitrogen balance and creates niacin, which is essential in creating the neurotransmitter serotonin, the hormone melatonin and spirit molecule Dimethyltryptamine (DMT). Danielle Haak says in "Tryptophan: Structure, Sources and Side Effects" that, "When the body doesn't get enough tryptophan, it can't make serotonin, which leads to increased feelings of depression."

SEROTONIN

Serotonin is a neurotransmitter known as the body's "feel good" hormone formed by the amino acid called tryptophan. It assists with many bodily functions including; appetite control, mood, endocrinal secretion regulation, learning and memory.

MELATONIN

Melatonin is a hormone produced primarily by the pineal gland. It assists with the regulation of sleep-wake cycles, is a potent antioxidant and positively interacts with the immune system.

PINOLINE

Pinoline is an extremely powerful, antimicrobial, anti-inflammatory, anti-aging and anti-cancer antioxidant. Pinoline is formally known as "6-methoxy-1,2,3,4-tetrahydro-β-carboline", usually abbreviated as "6-MeO-THBC" or "pinoline", taken from the words "pineal beta-carboline". It is a methoxylated (modified by the addition of one or more methoxy groups) Tryptoline produced in the pineal gland during the metabolism of melatonin. The most amazing thing about pinoline is its ability to promote cell health and production in the nervous system (neurogenesis).

In "A Proposed Mechanism for the Visions of Dream Sleep", Dr. J.C. Callaway speculates that the endogenous production of DMT and pinoline play a distinct role in dream phenomena. Funnily enough, these two fascinating compounds are also the major components of the shamanic elixir known as "Ayahuasca".

MEXAMINE

Formally known as "5-Methoxytryptamine" (5-MT), Mexamine is produced via the deacetylation (removal of an acetyl group from the molecule) of melatonin in the pineal gland. Mexamine helps to decrease appetite.

BENZODIAZEPINE

Commonly known as "benzos", benzodiazepine is a sedative that allows the mind and body to relax. It enhances the effect of the neurotransmitter "gamma-aminobutyric acid" (GABA) resulting in the secretion of other useful biochemicals that aid the body in rest, regeneration and rejuvenation.

TRYPTOLINE

Tryptoline is an antioxidant neurotransmitter, also known as tetrahy-dro-β-carboline. It is a natural organic derivative of beta-carboline. It is an alkaloid chemically related to tryptamine.

LUCIFERIN-BINDING PROTEIN (LBP)

Luciferins are light-emitting compounds that generate what is known as bioluminescence (living light). They are a class of small-molecule substrates that are oxidized in the presence of a luciferase (an enzyme) to produce light energy.

> "At the molecular level, bioluminescence is produced when chemicals, or "substrates" intermingle at the right time and place: luciferin, luciferase, and a third player, oxygen."
> Luminescentlabs.org

Although the chemicals listed here are all fundamental in the physical process of preserving the Sacred Secretion, particular attention should be drawn to DMT and Luciferin-binding protein (LBP) due to their marked capabilities which are truly "magical". It is these "magical" chemicals, along with Divine Energy flowing through us that allow us to "feel" the material experience of enlightenment.

An incredible parallel that can be highlighted here is between the Luciferin-binding Protein (LBP) and "Lucifer" the demon, devil or fall-en-angel. When oxidized by the enzyme Luciferase, LBP becomes a light-producing substance known as a bioluminescent - the same substance that gives fireflies their magical glow.

Lucifer is commonly known as the rebellious archangel identified with

Satan, and less commonly, but more realistically, Venus the "morning star". Belief that Lucifer was the "proper" name for Satan began with its use in the Bible to translate the Greek word, "Phosphorus". However, it is a mistake to identify Lucifer and Satan as being the same. The true translation of "Phosphorus" is: "a number of substances that exhibit luminescence when struck by light of certain wavelengths" and Venus was named after it.

This is indeed interesting because the embodiment of certain "wavelengths" can assist in melatonin transformation. Having explained the production process of DMT and other Sacred Secretion chemicals let's move on to discuss how and why this transformational "upgrade" occurs.

We've already touched upon the fact that deep, nourishing breaths can reduce carbon dioxide in the blood thus facilitating melatonin enhancement. So too does fasting or eating only when hungry due to the fact that carbon dioxide is produced during digestion. Also, the wavelengths produced by being calm and joyful will allow the pituitary gland to release other hormones such as oxytocin and vasopressin that facilitate melatonin upgrades. Exposure to situations that evoke strong, negative visceral responses such as anger, fear or guilt within us will cause the body to secrete apposing chemicals that will inevitably cause the entire process of melatonin enhancement to slow down and even stop.

This is largely due to the fact that emotions are vibratory frequencies (wavelengths) and are ultimately what cause all biological activity within our body's (more on this throughout the book). When a "healthy", meaning not calcified (to be explained later), pineal gland is exposed to a positive environment of love, health, truth, peace and joy it can tune into those high vibratory frequencies and upgrade the chemistry of tryptophan and subsequently melatonin. The higher the vibratory frequency the more substantial the chemical enhancements and the more significant the "felt" experience of raising the Sacred Secretion.

The God-given ability to enhance melatonin within our body through our thoughts, actions and behaviours is truly a gift and shows how "fearfully and wonderfully made" (Psalm 139:14) we really are.

Within the body, the highest volumes of DMT travel in our cerebrospinal fluid (CSF). For this reason, we will be following the course of CSF throughout the body in order to highlight the pathway and transformation of this incredible "Spirit Molecule".

CHAPTER 6

Jesus Christ – The Celestial Prophecy, The Human Man, The Spiritual Consciousness and The Seed.

"For no one can build on any other foundation
than that which is laid, which is Yahusha Mashiak"
2 KOR 3:11 (BYNV)

The personal name for Jesus in the Hebrew Bible is "Yahusha" - pronounced Yah-who-sha. Strong's Blue Letter Bible entry H3467 states that:

> "Yâsha' is the primitive root, meaning "to be open, wide or free, that is, (by implication) to be safe; causatively to free or succour: to defend, deliver, help, preserve, rescue, to bring or to have salvation, to save, or to be a Saviour, or to get victory."

The Torah Institute and the book "Fossilized Customs" by Lew White declare that "Yahusha" is the most accurate transliteration of the name given to the Messiah. Since "Yah" is the "I am" of God, the father or the heavenly creator, Yahusha means; "I am he who rescues", "I am the saviour" etc.

The name Christ comes from the Hebrew word, "Mashiach" and the Greek word, "Khristos" meaning "anoint or smear with oil" and was used for anyone who was or who was perceived as being "enlightened". It is a title similar to Doctor, Lord or President. There is also some evidence to show that the Sanskrit word for Christos means: "clear as crystal". This could pertain to the understanding of the Sacred Secretion known by the Essenes as, "the perfect light (crystal) body," by the Christians as the "resurrection body" and or by the Jewish Kabbalists as the "Merkabah". Also, it would be a major omission not to note the similarity between the Greek "Khristos" and the Hindus "Krishna," the latter of which who existed before the others.

For this study however, I will simply suggest that within the creative layers described in chapter 4, the name Jesus Christ pertains to the perfect expression of God's love as the Spiritual Sun, a physical man <u>and</u> the rescuing seed.

"Primitive Christians, the Essenes, fully realized and taught the great truth that Christ was a substance, an oil or ointment contained especially in the spinal cord, consequently in all parts of the body, as every nerve in the body is directly or indirectly connected with the wonderful "River that flows out of Eden (the upper brain) to water the garden."

(Page 89) "God-Man: The Word Made Flesh" by George W Carey & Ines Eudora Perry

Don't let the analytical brain or carnal mind assume that just because

Jesus Christ is a "substance" or Sacred Secretion in the microcosm (body), that he wasn't also a physical-historical being who God rose from the dead in order to highlight, parallel or mirror this phenomenon. That would be placing a limit on how we perceive God's limitless power and would deny the multi-levels of God's wonderful creation.

> "A few learned Christian mystics among our British The-osophists included, deny but the Gospel Jesus — who is not an historical personage — but believe in the *idea* of an "ideal Christ" [or fully initiated adept]. Others are inclined to see the real Jesus in the adept mentioned in the oldest Talmudic as well as some Christian books and known as Jeshu ben-Panthera."
>
> "Jesus Ben Pandira, the Historical Christ" www.Philaletheians.co.uk

I, myself do believe that there is/was a historical person, Yahusha (Jesus) also known as Jesus Ben (son of) Pandira, teacher of the Essenes, born of immaculate conception a phenomenon recently proven to be a scientific possibility by Dr Alfred Byrne of Cambridge University). I also understand that the Microcosmic Christ is a "seed" or "substance" within the human body and that metaphysically Jesus Christ is the "I" in man, the "self", the directive power raised to "divine understanding" – the "I Am" identity of mankind. But since the physical life of Jesus cannot be empirically, objectively proven, outside of Biblical texts, I would like to suggest that, regardless of whether you decide to believe in the "person" of Christ or, prefer to think of him as a fictional character, his impact on the collective consciousness of humankind has been vast. Just as God intended; Christ's Spirit, persona, teachings and influence have still, by this time, had the same profoundly wonderful effect on humanity either way. His story has still touched us individually, emotionally and physiologically and if we follow Christ's teachings of unconditional love and peace we will be illumined.

> "To the Christian Theosophist, Jesus is a manifestation of Adonai, the Christ, or Christ Spirit, of whom there have been many incarnations on this Earth, and he (Jesus) is the fullest and most perfect. They believe him to be the guiding protector of this planet during His particular cycle, and that coming into it, He comes to His own, not only to instruct, but to give a fresh impulse at the end of certain periods of six hundred years, called Naroses, or Naronic cycles, and if, therefore, it could be proven by those who assert that Jesus is only a mythical, and not an historical personality, the whole theory of the Naronic Cycles, founded on Astronomical science, which is to be found in the doctrines of every ancient country, all over the civilized world, would fall to the ground, and prove after a million of ages to be but a vain delusion."
>
> (Page 122) "The Secret History of the World" by Jonathan Black

Assigning this information to the four layers of creation described in chapter 4, puts Jesus Christ in all four layers:

LAYER ONE: GOD – Divine Energy - created all things and is in all things.

LAYER TWO: SPACE – Not only do the star constellations mirror or foretell the coming Messiah plus details of his birth and life, but the sun is the planet of Christ and Michael is the archangel of the sun. (research "Gospel in the Stars" for further information)

LAYER THREE: PHYSICAL HUMAN – Christ is a living person (or fictional character depending on your belief) who raised the collective consciousness of the world by overcoming evil.

LAYER FOUR: SPIRITUAL HUMAN – Christ's resurrection occurs within the body when God's divine energy transmutes and melatonin upgrades.

CHAPTER 7

The Solar Seed

"For the Lord God is a Sun and a Shield"

Psalm 84:11 (KJV)

E arth is surrounded by a protective environment, namely; the magnetosphere. The magnetosphere or "shield" deflects a stream of charged particles (Solar Seed Energy) from the Sun toward earth. This supersonic stream of charged particles is known as "solar wind".

The solar wind is a plasma that consists of ionized hydrogen (electrons and protons) with an 8% component of helium (alpha particles) and trace amounts of heavy ions and atomic nuclei with kinetic energy between 0.5 and 10 keV. Contained within the solar-wind plasma is the "interplanetary magnetic field" (IMF), also known as the "Heliospheric Magnetic Field" (HMF) which encompasses all of the planets within it and is the means by which the Sun interacts with planetary magnetospheres. The IMF transmits charged particles through the heliosphere or region of space that is dominated by the Sun. The IMF reveals an array of waves, discontinuities, and turbulence, which give hints to the solar wind formation process. This means that the sum of all energetic stellar and planetary influences encapsulated in each charged particle or Solar Seed, is transmitted into our human organism, specifically the solar plexus energy centre located in the stomach, by the sun.

> "The word gold comes from "or" - a product of the sun's rays or breath of life. Life or Spirit breathed into man precipitates brain cells and Gray matter which create or build the fluids and structure of physical man. "Or" is the seed (substance) as in W-OR-D or L-OR-D. "In the beginning was the word (seed) and the word was God", God means power."
>
> (Page 56) "God-Man: The Word Made Flesh" by George W. Carey and Ines Eudora Perry

The scientific facts regarding the Solar Wind are reflected by the studies of sacred geometry in which the Solar Seed is known as the "Seed of Life" and is made up of seven interlocking circles that represent the aspects (planetary influences) of the solar system and is also known as the "Genesis Pattern". The central circle represents the sun and the other six represent the remaining classical planets. Together these seven planets are the "Elohim", the "heavenly bodies" and the "seven sages"; huge in the macrocosm or space and miniscule within the microcosm or each Solar Seed. The ancients knew that God had given them prominence and power - hence why the seven days of the week are named after them: Sunday (Dies Solis) = "Sun"day, Monday (Dies Lunae) = "Moon"day, Tuesday (Dies Martis) = "Mars"day, Wednesday (Dies Mercurii) = "Mercury"day, Thursday (Dies Jovis) = "Jupiter"day, Friday (Dies Veneris) = "Venus"day and Saturday (Dies Saturni) = "Saturn"day.

For the sake of simplicity, let's summarise by saying that the Solar wind is a gust full of "Seeds of Life" or "Solar Seeds" containing stellar and planetary properties that enter the human organism at the Solar Plexus energy centre in the stomach.

Again, this process illustrates the glorious layers of creation and how the human organism corresponds with them:

LAYER ONE: GOD – Divine Energy - created everything and is in everything.

LAYER TWO: The sun emits Solar Seeds containing energetic planetary influences that deflect through the magnetosphere toward earth

LAYER THREE: The Solar Seeds are absorbed into the human organism via the Solar Plexus energy centre, also known as, the androgynous brain or the stomach brain.

LAYER FOUR: The Solar Seed contains all of the properties and information needed to fructify the Christ-Lunar-Germ seed once a month.

In the Bible the birth place of Jesus Christ is Bethlehem. "Beth" is a Hebrew letter meaning "house" and "lehem" means "bread"; this "house of bread" refers to the Solar Plexus. Scripture also tells us that the "seed to live by" proceedeth out of the mouth of God and that the mouth of God is also the source of all creation. "In the beginning was the word and the word was with God and the word WAS God." **John 1:1 (KJV)**

> "It is written, Man shall not live by bread alone,
> but by every word (seed) that proceedeth out of
> the mouth of God."
>
> **Matthew 4:4 (KJV)**

This scripture uses the term "word" as a metaphor for the word "seed", but make no mistake the actual "words" of God are equally as powerful as the "seeds" and depending on your perception are indeed one and the same because, as God's word is the initiation of all creation, so is the seed or nuclei in ALL the layers of creation:

> "Being born again, not of corruptible seed, but of
> incorruptible, by the word of God, which liveth
> and abideth for ever."
>
> **1 Peter 1:23 (KJV)**

> "Now the parable is this: The seed is the word
> of God."
>
> **Luke 8:11 (KJV)**

Just as the Sun is our external source of energy, the Solar plexus is our internal energy source. It is known esoterically as the "stomach brain" and the branches or roots of 12 cranial nerves (12 disciples) connecting to the brain are present here. It is the energy centre connected to the digestive system or Enteric Nervous System (ENS), known scientifically as the "second brain". The brain in our head and our "stomach brain" are physically connected by the Vagus nerve (Tree of Life), the nerve plexuses and the spinal cord (including the CSF), and subtly connected by the other six energy centres (Chakras).

CHAPTER 8

Xenogenesis – Nuclear Fusion

"And to thy seed, which IS Christ"

Galatians 3:16 (KJV)

One way to describe and understand the Sacred Secretion is through the study of Xenogenesis. In Revelation 7:4 we are told that, "there were sealed an hundred and forty and four thousand of all the tribes of the children of Israel", which also refers to the 144,000 DNA genes within the human organism. DNA is essentially comprised of five elements which each correspond directly to the well-known environmental elements: Carbon (Earth), Hydrogen (Water), Oxygen (Air), Nitrogen (Fire) and Phosphorus (Ether).

> "Xenogenesis is a spontaneous regeneration and transfiguration of the RNA DNA generations, thus the unique production of an organism that is altogether and permanently unlike the parent."
>
> Collins Dictionary

In the study of Xxenogenesis (the double "X" is not a mistake here), the "Christ (lunar germ) Seed" is the inactive RNA DNA (Ribonucleic acid) in the human organism and Xenogenesis-nuclear-fusion is the union of the "Christ-Lunar-Germ-Seed (RNA DNA – Anti Matter)" to the "Solar Seed (Matter)" and is the promised redeemer from death.

The Solar-Seed has one opportunity per month to impregnate or fructify the Christ-Lunar-Germ-Seed. When, the Moon (x) plus the Sun (+) come together they equal the eight-pointed star of the Essenes (*) overcoming the enmity that was between them. Accomplishing this at the specific time laid out by the creator's calendar is the immaculate conception of the Christ spirit into the mortal physical being.

Ribonucleic acid (RNA DNA) is an essential polymeric molecule. Its biological roles are in the coding, decoding, regulation and expression of genes. Similar to DNA, RNA DNA is a nucleic acid, these, along with lipids, proteins and carbohydrates, constitute the four major macromolecules imperative in the creation of all life forms.

DNA is a transmitter of light and codes for traits such as eye colour, but without RNA the genetic message would not be able to exit the cell in order to produce proteins.

There are three types of RNA:

1. Messenger RNA (MRNA) carries messages out of the nucleus to the Ribosome based off of the DNA.

2. Transfer RNA (TRNA) transfers the message to the cells and carries amino acids (building blocks of protein).

3. Ribosomal RNA (RRNA) is a component of Ribosome which makes protein.

To summarise, DNA is inside the nucleus and RNA is responsible for protein synthesis. There are two steps in protein synthesis 1, transcription (transcribing the DNA into a message) and 2, translation (brings the amino acids together to build protein). The MRNA tells the TRNA which amino acids to bring. RNA production happens by a:

> "special kind of metabolism involving proteins and macromolecules which are required for the growth of the synapses connectivity to nerve cells and for INCREASE IN MEMBRANE AND CHEMICAL TRANSMISSION. Thus, the existing synaptic connectivity becomes hyperactive and more efficient, or THERE IS A GROWTH OF NEW SYNAPSES."
>
> (Page 158) "Eternal Drama of Souls, Matter and God" by Jagdish Chander

These two "seeds", which, by default are in atomic enmity against one another can only fuse together once per month by the process of Xenogenesis-nuclear-fusion, when, by the power of limitless love the two seeds are electromagnetically drawn together.

> "Nicholas Cozzi PhD's research group at the University of Wisconsin in Madison has been investigating the gene that codes for the enzyme INMT RNA DNA, critical to the synthesis of endogenous DMT, and has discovered high levels of activity in the retina, spinal cord, and pineal gland. At first, INMT RNA DNA (the gene which is imperative for DMT production and activation) was not

detectable using standard Northern Blot Analysis. It is suspected that the INMT RNA DNA is inducible. This means that it is a dormant gene **whose expression is either responsive to environmental changes or a specific signal.**"

"The Chemistry of Consciousness" by Doctor Barker and Doctor Borjigin

CHAPTER 9

DNA

"And he dreamed, and behold a ladder set up on
the earth, and the top of it reached to heaven:
and behold the angels of God ascending and
descending on it."

Genesis 28:12 (KJV)

Firstly, its compelling to note that within the composition of the name of the book "Genesis" is the word, "genes" from the Greek root "Pan" meaning "all". Would it be too outlandish to nickname the book of Genesis, "The Book of Genes?" Or perhaps, "The Book of All?"

Genes contain DNA (deoxyribonucleic acid). DNA makes up human chromosomes and there is no denying that the shape of DNA resembles a ladder. This is one of many parallels to be drawn between Biblical Scripture and human physiology. Let's break it down a little further. If DNA is the "ladder", then RNA (ribonucleic acid) is the "messenger" in each half (vertical side) of the ladder - with half of each "rung" attached. Meaning that each "rung" is one nucleotide.

A nucleotide is a basic building block of RNA and therefore DNA.

Each nucleotide is made up of a combination of five elements:

1. Hydrogen (water)

    Specifically: Hydrogen bonds / Nucleic acid hydration

2. Nitrogen (fire)

    Specifically: Cytosine and Thymine (both Pyrimidines) and Adenine and Guanine (both Purines)

3. Carbon (earth)

    Specifically: Carbon atoms appear inside the sugary backbone of the nucleic acid

4. Oxygen (air)

    Specifically: Oxygen atoms appear in the nitrogenous bases, sugar, and phosphates of the nucleotides.

5. Phosphorus (ether)

    Specifically: Phosphate groups (phosphorus and oxygen) are attached to the sugar molecules; "Ribose" in RNA and "Deoxyribose" in DNA.

These five elements are the very framework of existence, the Sun for example - made mostly from hydrogen gives us the light and warmth that we need to live and the sugar molecule in DNA (Deoxyribose) is a five-sided pentose, also crucial for every function in the human organism.

Deoxyribose shares similar characteristics to the "Sacred Secretion" by what is biblically known as "Manna". According to Scripture there was a golden pot of Manna in the Ark of the Covenant, but what exactly was "Manna"? According to Exodus 16:35 "the children did eat manna forty years" and John 6:31 says "He gave them bread from heaven to eat." Exodus 16:31 offers a slightly more detailed description, "And the house of Israel called the name thereof Manna: and it was like coriander seed, white; and the taste of it was like wafers made with honey." This particular Scripture is really interesting because coriander seeds are tiny spheres that literally look like molecules, perhaps they were in fact molecules of Deoxyribose.

This mysterious "Manna" that looked like molecules and was a brown ("bdellium" Numbers 11:7) colour, was able to sustain people in the wilderness for an exceptionally long period of time. Also, in the book of Exodus we begin to see how it was transformed or transmuted alchemically into something even more potent, much like successfully preserved Sacred Secretion:

> "And when the dew that lay was gone up, behold,
> upon the face of the wilderness there lay a small
> round thing, as small as the hoar frost on the
> ground"
>
> **Exodus 16:14 (KJV)**

See how the Manna begins as "dew" but transforms into something bearing resemblance to "Hoar Frost"? This is really interesting because the word "crystal" comes from the Greek word "kryos" meaning frost and scientifically speaking, the Calcite Crystals inside the human pineal gland play a crucial part in the preservation of the Sacred Secretion - as will be seen later in this book.

> "For by him were all things created, that are in
> heaven, and that are in earth, visible and invis-
> ible, whether they be thrones, or dominions, or
> principalities, or powers: all things were created

41

> by him, and for him: And he is before all things,
> and by him all things consist (hold together)."
> **Colossians 1:16-17 (KJV)**

Aside from the likely existence of "Manna" within each nucleotide, DNA can also be likened to God's divine energy due to the fact that without DNA nothing living can be created. At this current time in history it seems as though DNA is returning to its original divine composition which is what is allowing our individual and collective consciousness to positively progress.

Zooming out on the focal point of DNA our biological design shows the presence of Laminin. Astoundingly laminin is shaped like a cross. Each laminin protein (cell-adhesion molecule) is part of what makes up the foundational network for most cells and organs. Laminin is vital for the maintenance and survival of tissues. You could say that if the God of creation is within our DNA then laminin protein is the Christ-adhesive that holds us together.

Whether speaking in terms of Christianity, Mysticism or Gnosticism the cross has been linked to many things, for example: the Kabbalistic human body, the point where the vagus nerve crosses the medulla oblongata, the burden of sin and the most exciting of all: the central axis of the universe where the physical world is theorized to meet the spiritual realm. There may well be truth in all of these interpretations because within the majestic layers of God's creation it's amazing to see reflections of things in different areas of the microcosm and macrocosm; materially, spiritually and mentally. Although, historians do argue that no empirical evidence that Jesus's body was hung on a cross appears until at least 300 years after his death. It was Constantine who promoted the cross symbol when he became an apostate Christian in the fourth century. The scholarly consensus as to the reason for this is that Constantine wanted to make it easier for pagans to accept Christianity. If this is all true it makes the fact that the Bible teaches against devotion to pagan symbols (2 Corinthians 6:16-18 KJV) truly questionable.

One final observation regarding DNA shows that the number of turns in a complete sequence of human DNA equals 33. Further discussions within this book will reveal the poignancy of this number.

CHAPTER 10

The Claustrum

"The claustrum is a thin, irregular, sheet-like neuronal structure hidden beneath the inner surface of the neocortex in the general region of the insula. Its function is enigmatic."

"Philosophical Transactions of the Royal Society of London, Series B, Biological Sciences" by Francis Crick and Christof Koch

Using modern science as their basis, Crick and Koch deliberate that the tiny Claustrum is quite likely the seat of all consciousness in the human body. Using an imaging technique whilst probing individual neurons inside the Claustrum, they saw that a neuron inside it branches out and extends around the entire circumference of the brain, much like a "Crown of Thorns," and confirmed it to be the most well-connected part of the brain. The claustrum sends and receives information from almost all areas of the cortex. This information was further quantified by the findings of a group of researchers from George Washington University who found that the claustrum can act like an on-off switch for consciousness. While experimenting on a woman suffering from epilepsy, claustrum stimulation sent her into a near-catatonic state.

This established the claustrum as the likely receptor of "life energy" from our Divine Creator, whom for simplicity I will refer to as God. Rest assured that some of the multitude of names used for God will be mentioned in one respect or another later in the book.

This "life energy" or consciousness is referred to as many different things: "Esse" (Latin), "To be" (English), "Luminiferous Aether", "Source", "Prana". For the purpose of this book I will be using the term "divine energy" because I comprehend this "life energy" as being the divine gift of life from God and of God.

Since the Claustrum is the physical body's point of connection to consciousness and divine energy, it can be said that, in turn, the Claustrum is orchestrating, or facilitating every other mechanism within the body; big and small – including the secretions made by our glands which will be studied in detail throughout this book. Shaped like a tiny Santa hat the Claustrum literally brings the gift of life to our entire body.

CHAPTER 11

Pia Mater

"But whosoever drinketh of the water that I shall
give him <u>shall never thirst</u>; but the water that I
shall give him shall be in him a well of water
<u>springing up into everlasting life</u>."

John 4:14 (KJV)

Vital to the process of the Sacred Secretion is the "Pia Mater" which interestingly means, "tender mother" in Latin. The Pia Mater literally births the Cerebrospinal Fluid (living water) in which the DMT travels.

"The Pia Mater is the innermost and most vascular layer of
the meninges and is "impermeable to fluid which enables
it to <u>contain and circulate</u> cerebrospinal fluid (CSF)".
[Video] "Meninges of the Brain" by Ken Hub.

To further bolster the Biblical parallel between the Virgin Mother and the Pia Mater, it is exciting to see that there are two other "Maters" (mothers) involved in CSF production and circulation completing the three-in-one system of the cranial meninges. Firstly, there is the Dura Mater (Tough

Mother); the Biblical Virgin Mary was certainly "tough". She endured physical stress, trauma and bore the brunt of ridicule and accusations against her son, Jesus. Secondly, the Arachnoid Mater (Spider Mother), also known as the "subarachnoid space" carries, supports and protects the CSF throughout its entire journey just as Mary did for Jesus.

Once again, this highlights the magical potential realised by successfully preserving the Sacred Secretion. In so doing, our inner CSF chemistry ("living water" John 4:10) allows us to triumph over self-destructive tendencies. If the CSF is abused and neglected, we are weak and negative, but if it is nurtured and transmuted it is healing and rejuvenating.

The individual who lets him or herself become defeated by negative thoughts, gestures and or actions finds himself in a depressed and unstable frame of mind. In this state the body has become submerged in "troubled waters" (CSF rife with negative hormone secretions) and thus, of course the physical condition is affected. Additional details will be given later in this book.

Whereas when we are compassionate and loving the resulting positive mental and emotional states will be reflected in a healthy physiology. This is the manifestation of the natural law of cause and effect. We reap what we sow. So, let us remember that God is Love and the ultimate Healer and so when we are loving we become attuned, through resonance, with the perfection of God and manifest health in body and mind.

This water or CSF can also dissolve unhelpful and negative memories or thought patterns within us, just as the Great Biblical Flood washed away debilitating conditions and habits from the race that it obliterated.

CHAPTER 12

Vital Fluids

"He that believeth on me, as the scripture hath said, <u>out of his belly shall flow rivers of living water</u>."

John 7:38 (KJV)

Cerebrospinal Fluid (CSF) is powerful and vital. It is a clear, colourless liquid that surrounds and protects the Vagus Nerve and Central Nervous System (CNS). CSF bathes the brain and spine in nutrients and eliminates waste products.

CSF is the physical counterpart of the "river of life" that proceeds from the throne of God and is the divine energy, spirit flow or "Ruach", whose symbol is fire. CSF has been referred to as "liquid light" and the medium for "the breath of light" (Randolph Stone, founder of Polarity Therapy). Alchemy explains the process of the Sacred Secretion as the turning of Lead into Gold by the process of heat or fire. The Holy Spirit is often associated with or even described as fire and Cerebrospinal fluid (CSF) is a clear, highly conductive (electrical) liquid. Its high electric conductivity is one of the reasons that its influence within the body is so significant. Dr Randolph Stone said that: "the soul swims in the CSF and the CSF is a conveyer and storage field for ultrasonic light energy."

CSF flows around the brain and spinal cord by two pumping mechanisms; the occiput at the top of the spinal column and the sacral pump at the bottom.

Diaphragmatic breathing, such as is used in the practise of Kundalini, activates the CSF sacral pump at the bottom of the spine. This occurs as the dome shaped diaphragm muscle contracts down on the sacrum on an in breath, which pumps CSF up the spinal cord and into the brain. A succession of these contractions stimulates both pumps and encourages or strengthens their ability after the practice.

Meditation and sleep also improve the flow of CSF through the body by calming the glands in the brain and allowing the lower and upper CSF pumps to work in harmony with one another. In fact, scientists have found that during sleep there is as much as a 60% increase of CSF in the interstitial compartment (space around cells), once again aiding melatonin enhancements, cell health and production by increasing the convective exchange of CSF and interstitial fluid.

CSF is saline and alkaline and contains a high percentage of sodium chloride. It is derived from blood plasma and is fascinatingly similar to it with the exception that CSF is nearly protein-free compared with plasma and has some different electrolyte levels. They are both composed of ionized sodium, ionized chlorine, ionized magnesium, ironized calcium, ironized potassium and ironized heavy carbon, due to the way it is produced, CSF has a higher chloride level than plasma. Biblically speaking one could surmise that if the symbol for CSF is "living water" or the water within rivers, the symbol for blood could be "sea water".

Seawater is also of a significantly similar composition to CSF and blood plasma. Perhaps this is why Bible authors were inspired to use it as a symbol for these powerful bodily fluids. It's extraordinary how Scripture can be understood in terms of both the macrocosm and the microcosm.

> "Or who shut up the sea with doors, when it brake
> forth, as if it had issued out of the womb?"
> **Job 38:8 (KJV)**

Seawater is the only substance that combines all the physical and chemical properties that enable the emergence, continuation and development of life. Plato believed that seawater could heal all illnesses. Both seawater and blood plasma have the ability to balance or return homeostasis to the body:

> "For the life of the flesh is in the blood"
> **Leviticus 17:11**

Thalassotherapy was discovered by Plato and is basically seawater therapy. It studies the phenomenon and scientific explanation of seawater and its healing properties. I recommend reading about Rene Quinton's blood plasma, sea water related experiments and revelations as they are truly inspired.

CHAPTER **13**

Sperm and Prostate Fluid

"While dealing with the forms assumed by man, we must briefly notice those vital secretions which form the physical conditions for re-production of his kind. The seminal fluids are the most ethereal of all physical secretions and contain the very quintessence of man."

(Page 36) [Mysteries of Sex] "The Light of Egypt" By Thomas H Burgoyne

While explaining the "Christ Seed" it is important to discuss the physical male "Semen" and female equivalent, "prostate fluid" both of which are ejaculated during the climax of a sexual experience. These seminal fluids contain concentrations of minerals and elements that are integral for brain function and nerve health.

If the physical seminal fluids are not ejaculated, they can then mature and their spiritual essence, also known as Ojas can travel to the cerebro-spinal fluid (CSF) where it will be carried to the brain.

The word "Semen" wasn't used for human sperm until the 1800's. It comes from the Hebrew word "Shemen", meaning oil, the Greek word

"Semnos" meaning, "honour" and the Latin word "Serere" meaning, "to sow". The verb root "se" simply means, "set apart" just like Christ was. When the sensual part of sense consciousness is eliminated, meaning that sexual urges diminish and are replaced by pure thoughts the body will begin to express holiness and move toward "perfection".

When scripture tells us not to squander our "seeds" it is referring to the integral spiritual substance within the seminal fluids. Thought draws the "substance" to the spinal cord. The fatal spilling of this "substance" causes billions of solar seeds to be lost. Due to the fact that the body's impulses and the brain's neuropathways do not know the difference between a "real" experience and an imagined one, internal wastage of subtle sex energy can even occur as a result of "imagined sex" as well as interactive physical acts of sexual stimulation.

Mystics say that the sexual contraction that follows the spilling of physical semen gathers billions of "satanic" (Saturn-influenced) atoms which are transmitted into the subtle body via the root chakra. These "satanic" atoms fuel carnal desires by replacing the lost solar (Sun-influenced) atoms which are transmitted into the subtle body via the solar plexus chakra - where generation takes place. By lessening solar energy and heightening Saturn energy, mystics say that "evil" or the (d)evil is formed within us due to the imbalance of energy caused by ejaculation. However, when the vibratory frequency of true unconditional love is present during the act of "making love" and no measures (condoms, contraceptive pills etc.) are used to inhibit or dilute the sexual fluids this so "spilling" is prevented. Instead, the masculine and feminine complement one another - both physically and spiritually.

"When the sexual organism is evolved above the physical plane of its manifestation, the seminal fluids are absorbed by the magnetic constitution and the etherealised atoms to help build up the body of man. But when this is not so these seminal germs, if not passed off amid the other secretions from the body, live and germinate a swarm of elemental lifeforms which rob the organism of a portion of its vitality. To obey the laws of nature is the only safe and sure road to evolve the spiritual senses of the soul."

(Page 36) [Mysteries of Sex] "The Light of Egypt" by Thomas H Burgoyne

Scientifically speaking there are five known measurable benefits of semen retention:

1. Increased Serotonin levels

   The main importance of this first one has already been explained in Chapter 5. But just to recap: Serotonin is vital in DMT production and the enhancement of Melatonin.

2. Decreased Prolactin levels

   Excess Prolactin can cause various problems such as: depression and mood swings, anxiety and headaches and even weight gain.

3. Normal Dopamine levels

   Dopamine can be as beneficial in normal quantities as it can be detrimental in low or excess quantities. Too much dopamine drives addiction, compulsion and aggression whereas too little dopamine leads to apathy and the inability to love. However, a "normal" level of dopamine fuels healthy motivation, focus and excitement for life.

4. Increased Testosterone levels
    Good levels of testosterone promote healthy hair, skin and teeth
    - not to mention the mental benefits; self-confidence, focus and
    determination.
5. Increased brain Androgen Receptors (AR's)
    AR's allow your body to use testosterone.

You don't have to look far to learn of successful men who spoke openly of their preference to retain semen for increased focus and energy. Among the most famous ones are: Muhammad Ali, Steve Jobs, Kanye West, Pythagoras and Nikola Tesla.

> "When driven by [sexual] desire, men develop keenness
> of imagination, courage, will-power, persistence, and cre-
> ative ability unknown to them at other times. So strong
> and impelling is the desire for sexual contact that men
> freely run the risk of life and reputation to indulge it.
> When harnessed, and redirected along other lines, this
> motivating force maintains all of its attributes of keen-
> ness of imagination, courage, etc., which may be used as
> powerful creative forces in literature, art, or in any other
> profession or calling, including, of course, the accumu-
> lation of riches."
>
> (Page 261) "Think and Grow Rich" by Napoleon Hill

CHAPTER **14**

The Pineal Gland

"Jacob named the place Peniel because, he said, "I
saw God face-to-face and lived to tell the story."

Genesis 32:30

Associations: Male, Sun and Solar Fire, Gold & Sulphur, Electric, Joseph,
Lingam, Yang, Pine Cone, "Peniel" the place where Jacob met God, the
7th Chakra or Crown Chakra

Connected to: The Electric (+) Pingala Nadi

Physical Secretions: Melatonin

Symbolic Secretions: Frankincense (Pine-resin or the incense of priest-
hood), Honey

The Pineal gland has more blood flow per cubic volume than any other
organ and is surrounded or bathed in CSF. As our internal clock, the
Pineal gland regulates our circadian rhythms by producing melatonin (the
sleep chemical) and serotonin (the awake chemical). The release of these
chemicals relies among other things upon exposure to darkness (sunset
or eyes closing) and light (sunrise or eyes opening). When day turns to

night and we begin to get tired, the Pineal is busy converting Serotonin into Melatonin which is then released to induce sleepiness.

The moment of transference between these two states; sleep and awake is known as the transluminal phase or the hypnagogic state. Many incredibly successful people, Einstein, Thomas Edison and Aristotle for example are known to have purposefully induced the hypnagogic state in order to receive inspiration and gain clarity.

Hypnagogic dreams happen during this transluminal phase between sleep and awake and are very different to normal REM dreams. REM dreams usually have some kind of narrative, whereas hypnagogic dreams are more like random disassociated thoughts, images, sounds and sensations which come from the subconscious brain. Most commonly, people see abstract light patterns and auditory hallucinations such as voices.

Scientific research suggests that hypnagogic experiences are very useful in solving problems that require creative insight and throughout history prophecies, premonitions and visions have likely occurred as a result of the hypnagogic phenomenon.

> "Hypnagogia allows a loosening of egoic boundaries, openness, sensitivity and a fluid suggestion of ideas."
>
> "Hypnagogia: The Unique State of Consciousness Between Wakefulness and Sleep" by Andreas Mavromatis

In order to induce the transluminal state, Thomas Edison would deliberately fall asleep with a handful of steel ball bearings; as soon as his hand relaxed the balls would drop and wake him up just in time to write down whatever he experienced in hypnagogia. Nowadays there are "dreamcatchers" on the market created for this precise purpose.

In Chapter 5, "The Secretion: Physical Properties" we have already seen how melatonin and serotonin are constituents of DMT.

> "Recent research at the University of Toronto has shown that meditating on the Pineal gland using methods recommended by Indian yogis causes it to release a rush of melatonin, the secretion that causes us to have dreams and, in sufficient dosages, can also cause waking hallucinations."
>
> (Page 80) "The Secret History of the World" by Jonathan Black

Melatonin suppresses the adrenal "stress hormone" cortisol and therefore has a significant effect on mood, the immune system and the aging process.

Excessive production of the stress hormones "Cortisol" and "Epinephrine" can cause brain damage and problems in ALL other parts of the body – since the secretions of these hormones are caused by emotion, IT IS SCIENTIFICALLY PARAMOUNT FOR MENTAL AND PHYSICAL HEALTH to be peaceful, loving and forgiving, just as the Bible suggests.

The Pineal Gland consists of tiny calcite crystals that are composed of calcium, carbon and oxygen and are less than 20 microns in length. Due to their structure and piezoelectric properties, applying pressure to these crystals creates an electromechanical, biological transduction mechanism or simply put; an electrically charged information receiver and translator much like an antenna within the brain. This electrical charge generates an electromagnetic field that in turn receives and transmits information from other electromagnetic fields; such as people, plants and planets and translates the information into recognizable thoughts, images and ideas.

Breathing exercises and yoga help to encourage the piezoelectric function of the Pineal by increasing CSF flow, which raises to the Pineal and divides to flow all the way around it, pressurizing the calcite crystals and stimulating the Cilia. Cilia are tiny hairs (likened to oars or paddles) on the exterior of the Pineal and inner ventricular surfaces of the central CSF canal in the spinal cord.

> "It is proposed that they (Cilia) function to capture and guide endogenous photons that are transmitted across the ventricular spaces from opposing ependymal surfaces, and that they guide the direction in which photons are emitted from ependymal cells into the ventricular spaces."
>
> (Page 2) [Photon Emission] "Endogenous Light Nexus Theory of Consciousness" by Karl Simanonok

When the Calcite Crystals are pressurized, and the Cilia hairs are aroused the Pineal secretes the upgraded metabolites of melatonin (detailed in chapter 5) into the brain, which subsequently travel to the rest of the body causing a highly positive energising, purifying and healing effect throughout. Eventually this energy will return back up the spine, into the brain stem to the outer "shell" of the egg-like thalamus (nucleus reticularis) opening the gate of neural resonant traffic, where it relays messages to the cortex leaving us with the sense of awakening.

The more we become aware of our breath and spend time doing Yoga, meditation and practising positive breathing techniques the more efficient our internal antenna can become. Breath and effective CSF circulation are the most important elements for pineal activation and health. There is nothing else like Yoga for CSF acceleration and conditioning.

CHAPTER **15**

The Pituitary Gland

"Like newborn infants, long for the pure spiritual
milk, that by it you may grow up into salvation— "
1 Peter 2:2 (KJV)

Associations: Female, Moon, Air, Silver and Mercury, Magnet, Mary, Yoni, Yin, the "master gland", the 6th Chakra or Brow Chakra
Connected to: The Magnetic (-) Ida Nadi
Physical Secretions: Somatotropin (growth hormone), oxytocin ("the love hormone"), vasopressin (body fluid regulator)
Symbolic Secretions: Myrrh (contains sesquiterpene compounds that increase activity in the pineal, pituitary, and thalamus glands), Milk

Known as the "Master Gland", the Pituitary gland is tightly connected to the hypothalmus via blood and nerve pathways, which in turn activate the Pineal Gland. The Pituitary is located above the sphenoid sinus where CSF is secreted during high levels of excitement. The Pituitary gland has two lobes; anterior and posterior. Each lobe secretes a different set of hormones:

HORMONES OF THE ANTERIOR LOBE:

1. Growth Hormone (GH/Somatotropin) - stimulates muscle and bone development, the growth and division of cells and protein synthesis

2. Prolactin (PRL/Luteotropic) – stimulates milk production after child birth

3. Tropic (other endocrine gland assistors) Hormones:
   - Follicle-stimulating hormone (FSH) – assists the reproductive system
   - Luteinizing hormone (LH) – stimulates ovulation and testosterone production
   - Adrenocorticotropic hormone (ACTH) – stimulates the adrenal glands and cortisol balance
   - Thyroid stimulating hormone (TSH/Thyrotropin) - stimulates the thyroid gland to produce thyroxine (T4), and then tri-iodothyronine (T3) which stimulates the metabolism of almost every tissue in the body.

HORMONES OF THE POSTERIOR LOBE:

1. Oxytocin
2. Vasopressin

Both of which can independently and synchronously heighten feelings of trust, peace and empathy & reduce feelings of fear anxiety and aggression.

The hormones that the Pituitary gland produces also stimulate the activity of other endocrine glands in the physical body and subsequently their corresponding energy centres (Chakras) in the subtle body.

The physical Pituitary Gland is connected to the spiritual brow Chakra. The brow Chakra is assigned to large petals which represent the two lobes of the pituitary body.

> "Wherefore laying aside all malice, and all guile,
> and hypocrisies, and envies, and all evil speakings,
> as new-born babes, desire the sincere milk of the
> word, that ye may grow thereby: If so be ye have
> tasted that the Lord is gracious"
>
> **1 Peter 2 (KJV)**

The more efficient the Pineal Gland becomes in "upgrading" melatonin, the more the Pituitary gland is stimulated to secret oxytocin and vasopressin. The increased production and secretion of oxytocin causes a metabolic shift within the Vagus Nerve (more on this in Chapters 20 and 33), from sympathetic (stress mode) into parasympathetic (restorative mode) - meaning a lowering of cortisol levels and faster healing of wounds. Oxytocin makes the heart swell and heals past hurts beyond what we perhaps knew possible, not to mention giving a stronger capacity for forgiveness and unconditional love.

The increased production and secretion of vasopressin, which is an antidiuretic helps the body to retain its vital conductive fluids (CSF, blood and water) and therefore assists the entire process of preserving the Sacred Secretion.

CHAPTER 16

The Thalamus

"The light of the body is the eye: if therefore thine
eye be single; thy whole body shall be full of light."

Matthew 6:22

Associations: The Seed of existence, The Philosophers Stone, Lamp, Lamb (Aries)

Connected to: The Sushumna Nadi

Symbolic Association: The Alchemical Gold, Gold from the Wise Men

The seven stars of Orion are: Rigel, Betelgeuse, Bellatrix, Alnilam, Alnitak, Saiph and Mintaka. These 7 stars ARE paralleled in the microcosmic thalamus, the "Light of the World; the "Land of God" as the seven sensory cranial nerves:

1. The Olfactory – SENSE OF SMELL (first cranial – sensory only)

2. The Optic – SENSE OF SIGHT (second cranial – sensory only)

3. The Trigeminal – SENSATION IN THE FACE AND MOTOR FUNCTIONS SUCH AS CHEWING (fifth cranial – motor and sensory)

4. The Facial - CONTROLS THE MUSCLES OF FACIAL

EXPRESSION, AND FUNCTIONS IN THE CONVEYANCE OF TASTE SENSATIONS FROM THE ANTERIOR TWO-THIRDS OF THE TONGUE (seventh cranial – motor and sensory)

5. The Acoustic – TRANSMITS SOUND FROM THE INNER EAR TO THE BRAIN (eighth cranial – sensory only)

6. The Glossopharyngeal - CONNECTS TO THE BRAINSTEM AT THE UPPER MEDULLA, TRAVELS THROUGH THE BASE OF THE SKULL AT THE JUGULAR FORAMEN, AND ENDS IN THE MOUTH IN THE MUCOUS GLANDS, PALATINE TONSIL, AND THE BASE OF THE TONGUE. IT SPLITS INTO VARIOUS BRANCHES: THE TONSILLAR, TYMPANIC, STYLOPHARYNGEAL, CAROTID SINUS NERVE, LINGUAL, COMMUNICATION BRANCH TO THE VAGUS NERVE, AND A BRANCH TO THE BACK THIRD OF THE TONGUE (ninth cranial – motor and sensory)

7. The Vagus – THE LONGEST NERVE IN THE BODY REACH-ING FROM THE BRAIN TO THE BASE OF THE SPINE (tenth cranial – motor and sensory)

> "The activity of the human brain, which we have already seen to be filled and surrounded by a subtle humidity, causes an akasic precipitation, a brain 'dew' which is more of a luminous ether than a liquid. This 'dew,' however, is more tangible than a gas, and as the manna is said to have fallen from heaven, so this 'dew' of thought trickles down between the two hemispheres of the cerebrum and finally fills the third ventricle, which is the reservoir, so to speak, of this heavenly water. This 'dew' carries in

suspension, or as the alchemists might say, is 'tinctured' by the mental activity of the seven brain stars which form the northern constellation of man. Paracelsus thus sums up the mystery: 'The whole of the Microcosm is potentially contained in the Liquor Vitae, a nerve fluid—in which is contained the nature, quality, character and essence of beings.'"

(Page 73) [Salt of the Wise] "Nitrogeno 03: Making Gold" Autumn 2016, Fontana Editore

Beyond the microcosm, smaller still, there are another "7 stars", that is to say Electrons orbiting every nitrogen atom – see how God designed these corresponding layers so intricately and beautifully!

Along with the Pineal and Pituitary glands, the thalamus is included in the symbolic design of many sacred buildings and, it is of course, included in the caduceus symbol. This is because it is vital to the process of the Sacred Secretion; some call the Pineal, Pituitary and the Thalamus the "Real Holy Trinity" because when all three are in balance a synchronized or awakened state initiates within the brain.

Another layer of this spectacular trinity can be seen on a cellular level; the Neutron (Father) "One God and Father of all, who is above all, and through all, and in you all" Ephesians 4:6, the Proton (Son) situated to the right of the neutron "and the Son of man standing on the right hand of God." Acts 7:56 and the Electron (Holy Ghost) "But ye shall receive power, after that the Holy Ghost is come upon you." Acts 1:8.

Author of the book "Hypnagogia", Andreas Mavromatis, says that "The Thalamus is the source of all hypnagogic phenomena." The egg-shaped Thalamus has two lobes known as the "thalamic bodies", which are connected by the Massa Intermedia nerve (more recently known as Interthalamic Adhesion). In between the lobes is the Third Ventricle which just so happens to be filled with cerebrospinal fluid (CSF).

The Massa Intermedia or Interthalamic Adhesion close to the fornix is continuously fusing and re-fusing the thalamic bodies together creating a microcosmic version of the process of procreation; male influence and female influence = the fertilisation of the seeds within the CSF. It is this fusion that reflects spiritual rebirth and Jesus Christ rising from the dead.

> "Except a man be born again, he cannot see the
> kingdom of God."
>
> **John 3:3 (KJV)**

To summarize, when upgraded or pressurized CSF flows up the spinal cord to the brain stem, the cerebellum opens up to it through a cluster of nuclei known as the Reticular Formation, where it then meets the Thalamic Gate. The CSF passes through the Thalamic Gate and into the Thalamus, which relays signals to and from the aforementioned Seven Sensory Cranial Nerves and the Pineal - where, calcite crystals transform and stimulate the Pineal to secrete the upgraded chemicals examined in Chapter 5. The CSF then continues to the Neocortex creating gamma waves of 30Hz and above allowing for heightened perception.

The microcosmic Thalamus within the brain is linked to the constellations of Orion, Draco and the Fornax in the universal macrocosm.

CHAPTER **17**

Orion

"Canst thou bind the sweet influences of Pleiades,
or loose the bands of Orion?"

Job 38:31 (KJV)

Associations: Osiris or "The Gate of Heaven"
Associations to the 3 stars that form the belt: Three Wise Men, Three
Kings

In etymology the word "Orion" can be deduced to mean "electrically
charged gate". This gate channels electrically charged atoms (Ions) to
the Fornix of the brain. These Ions are also responsible for the electrical
charge within photons (light particles or solar seeds).

"The measuring attainment of the great pyramid would
indicate all substance of measure of the heavens and the
earth"

"The Secret Doctrine" Vol 1. by Madame Helena P. Blavatsky

The three Belt Stars of Orion are related to the Pineal, Pituitary and Thalamus:

1. Alnitak – Zeta Orionis
2. Alnilam – Epsilon Orionis
3. Mintaka – Delta Orionis

Orion's belt stars are also aligned to the majestically designed and executed Egyptian Pyramids which were measured with absolute precision to replicate the earth and its position in the universe. Here are just a few incredible facts:

The air shaft on the left side of the King's Chamber, which is positioned in total parallel to the Thalamus, points DIRECTLY to Alnitak in Orion and the air shaft on the right-side points directly to Thuban in Draco (The pole star of 3000BC).

The air shaft on the left side of the Queen's Chamber, which is positioned in total parallel to the Hyper Thalamus, points DIRECTLY to Sirius in Canis Major and the air shaft on the right points directly to Kawkab in Ursa Minor (The pole star of today).

Sirius also known as the "Dog Star" represents liberation, freedom and initiation. It is said that Sirius strongly influences events on the earthly plane. It is the magnetic energy that emanates from Sirius that changes the earths magnetism and causes pole shifts.

The star constellation that aligns perfectly to the centre of the King's Chamber is the Fornax - paralleled with the fornix in the brain.

CHAPTER **18**

The Fornix

"Straight is the crossing and narrow is the way that leads to it."

Epic of Gilgamesh 2000 BC

"Because strait is the gate, and narrow is the way, which leadeth unto life, and few there be that find it."

Matthew 7:14 (KJV) 1611 AD

Associations: The Tomb of Tutankhamun (Amun) also known as the "great amen" (biblically, Jesus is also amen), The King's Chamber of the Great Pyramid of Giza, the Fornax constellation

Whether following the King James Bible published in 1611 or studying ancient Mesopotamian texts such as "The Epic of Gilgamesh," the essence of the stories and their meanings remain the same – "life" can be found on the straight and narrow path, i.e. when balance and unconditional love are restored and upheld within our thoughts and actions.

The Fornix is an organ connected to the Pineal Gland by an attachment known as the "stria pinealis" meaning, "straight line to the Pineal." The Fornix folds over and is connected to the Foramen Commune Anterius.

Biblically, Jesus described Himself as: "the Amen, the faithful and true witness" (Rev. 3:14). "Amen" is used at the end of our prayers so as to say, "thank you" and affirm our faith that God will respond.

There's an interesting parallel here: "Amen" *is* Jesus; the connection between spirit and matter and the foramen (for "amen") arch connects the hemispheres. Found at the centre of the brain, the Fornix is a vaulted (tomb) or arched structure in the body which connects the left and right hemispheres.

During meditation our brain waves slow from Beta 14-30 Hz (awake, normal alert consciousness) to Alpha 9-13 Hz (physically and mentally relaxed), to Theta 4-8 Hz (deep meditation and or light REM sleep) and finally to Delta below 4 Hz (loss of bodily awareness).

It is compelling to see that the star at the centre of the Fornax constellation is named, "Delta" and of course, it is at this super calm Delta level of brain activity that the Hypnagogic state can take place allowing us to experience Gamma waves 30 Hz and above that allow a heightened sense of perception and access to the subconscious mind. The Fornix is the place where Christ consciousness awakens as the hemispheres connect.

It is a triangular area of white matter in the brain between the hippocampus (associated with memories, emotions and motivation) and the hypothalamus (responsible for automatic responses).

CHAPTER 19

33 Vertebrae

"Your neck is like the tower of David, built with
rows of stones on which are hung a thousand
shields, All the round shields of the mighty men."
Song of Solomon 4:4 (KJV)

Associations: Jacob's ladder, tower of David, 33 years of Christ, 33 Gods in the Vedic Religion, the macrocosmic "Central Axis of The Universe" also known as "Axis of Evil".

The name "vertebrae" comes from "verto" meaning to turn or to spin which reminds us of the swirling energy ascending the spine.

From the bottom upward, the spine is broken down into the following sections:

4 fused vertebrae known as "The Coccyx" - representing the physical, emotional, intellectual and spiritual levels of humanity.

5 fused sacral vertebrae known as "The Sacrum" - representing the 5 physical senses of man.

5 Lumbar vertebrae, representing the vital organs of the lower regions.

12 Thoracic vertebrae, representing 12 cranial nerves, 12 baskets etc.

7 Cervical vertebrae, representing the seven candles, energy centres or Chakras

There is an age-old discussion that begs the question whether or not it is a mere coincidence that Jesus is believed to have lived for 33 years, or that the Freemasons have 33 steps to reach enlightenment and astronomical measuring devices purposely set to 33 degrees? I'm sure I don't need to list the many Biblical references to 33, but a few to fuel your own personal research are: Genesis 46:15: "All the souls of his sons and his daughters were thirty-three", Leviticus 12:4: "And he shall continue thirty-three days in the blood of her cleansing", Numbers 33:39: "And Aaron was a hundred and thirty-three years old when he died in mount hor".

Perhaps it's just serendipity that the "Clavicula Salomonis," also known as the "codex of King Solomon's temple" shows how the structure and design of King Solomon's temple not only replicates the human body but also corresponds directly to prominent stars? The Clavicula Salomonis states that there are "thirty-three elements of the cosmic ruler of darkness" and these elements are then named: "Deception", "Strife", "Jealousy" etc. Each so-called "element" is a "demon" that must be overcome. King Solomon's story has also been allegorically linked to Kundalini enlightenment by Gnostics and his name means: "sun (Sol) creation (o) moon (mon)".

Despite there being no empirical evidence on the exact identity of Solomon in the Clavicula Salomonis, there are many similarities that suggest he is indeed the King Solomon of the Bible. Both are the son of King David and carry the seal referred to as the Star of David, which significantly has the gematric value of 33. Regardless of how these ideas are packaged or explained, it appears as though the 33 years of Christ always represent a holy quest to ascend or climb toward enlightenment by facing ourselves and taming our "demons" or destructive states of consciousness.

> "Jesus Christ lived for thirty-three years. The significance of this number is one of the oldest and most closely guarded secrets of esoteric philosophy. Thirty-three is the rhythm of the vegetative realm of the cosmos, the dimension that controls interactions between the spirit worlds and the material world."
>
> (Page 475) "The Secret History of the World" by Jonathon Black

The study of "Spatial Order" shows that the "Central Axis of The Universe" said to be located on or between the 33rd parallels is the connection between the sacred and secular or, spiritual and material planes. Thus, it can be suggested that the 33 vertebrae of the spine are the microcosmic reflection of the "Central Axis of The Universe."

This mythic cosmic centre is found at the point around which the sun rotates. Similar to the hands on a clock lines can be drawn through this centre point to highlight the four extremities of the sun's daily positions. Two of these extremities are located at either end of the first line, this is the spiritual axis, the solar positions are: "Zenith" – Midday, and "Nadir" – Midnight. This first axis is the "Central Axis of The Universe" and is conceived to have three levels: sky, earth and underworld. The other two extremities are located at either end of a second line, this is the earthly axis, the solar positions are: "East" – Sunrise, and "West" – Sunset.

These two lines create a cross, potentially the most significant of all crosses, it is called the "Quincunx". The five points of the Quincunx; Zenith, Nadir, East, West and Centre Point are known to be of equal importance and represent the earth and the cosmos, life and motion, the endless cycle of time and space.

You don't need to look far to read about a vast amount of observations that have been made relating to the 33rd north and south parallels. For example, many pyramids and temples are built along them. Furthermore, Atlantis and the Bermuda Triangle are among the sites where suggested paranormal activity occurs and are found along these circles of latitude.

This next topic of discussion is also relevant to chapters: 27 – The Sun, 28 – The Moon and 30 – The Timing. However, due to the correspondence with the number 33 I have decided to include it here.

A lunar year, 12 synodic months is approximately 354 days. A solar year is approximately 365 days. Therefore, the lunar and solar cycles are out of sync by 11 days each year (365 – 354). The term "epact" is used to describe this specific time difference. "Epact: the excess of the solar month above the lunar synodic month, and of the solar year above the lunar year of twelve synodic months".

After 3 years the lunar months are out of cycle with the solar year by about 33 days or 1 month. In total, it takes 33 years for the cycle of lunar years to get back to the original position – therefore the entire luni-solar cycle is 33 years.

In astrology it is known that the sun enters each zodiacal sign at the 30th degree, but due to its size it is not completely clear (within that sign) until the 33rd degree. This could be why the Bible says Jesus's ministry began at the age of 30 and ended at the age of 33.

CHAPTER 20

The Vagus Nerve

"There is a seed, or psycho-physical germ born in the, or out of, the solar plexus and this seed is taken up by the nerves or branches of the vagus nerve, and becomes "The Fruit of the Tree of Life"

Page 90 "God-Man: The Word Made Flesh" by George W. Carey and Ines Eudora Perry

The Vagus nerve is known metaphysically as the Tree of Life. Its longer name is: the Pneumogastric Nerve (pneumo meaning breath and gastric meaning stomach). The Vagus nerve is the tenth cranial nerve (CNX), part of the peripheral nervous system and is comprised from thousands of miles of distinct nerve pathways that work via the principle of electricity.

Nerves are often compared to wires due to the fact that they carry electricity in the form of nerve fluids through the body. Every emotion that we express is transmitted over the nerves to the brain where our internal biochemistry and secretions alter accordingly giving us a "felt" experience. The brain then translates the emotions into thoughts and the thoughts are what become our spoken words. Words are expressed from the vocal cords in the throat, in terms of Biblical symbolism this could be "Cana – place of reeds". Be they positive or negative, all words affect emotions, both the things we tell ourselves and the words we say to others. Therefore, a sort of perpetuating circle occurs: reaction (expressed emotion), biochemical alteration, thought (negative/positive), words (negative/positive) and so on. Thus, it is easy to see the importance of calm, balanced responses from the Spiritual Heart to not only raise our own vibration and potential for positive repercussions, but also, the collective vibration toward love and unity. Making the decision to react positively rather than negatively, calmly rather than explosively, kindly rather than aggressively etc. is something that we can all do. As the saying goes: "It is better to light a candle than to curse the darkness."

In the Microcosm, the metaphysical meaning of "Tree" is "nerve". Nerves are an expression of thoughts of unity; they connect thought centres. If we are able to place ourselves in the "garden" through the understanding and embodiment of the "I AM" then the tree of life in the solar plexus region has been contacted. From this centre there is the potential to bring forth only goodness and exercise authority over every aspect of our lives; body, mind and spirit. In Ezekiel 47:7, the trees growing on both sides of the river represent the nerves that radiate from the spinal column and connect the entire human organism through the CSF and nerve fluid. In the Macrocosm, trees signify a connection between heaven and earth (Genesis 2:9).

The Vagus nerve really is a Tree of Life, not only carrying breath to the lungs and its roots in the solar plexus, but also assisting CSF (Living waters) around the brain and through the spine. It is the pneumogastric tree's job to refine the substance every month, when a transmutation occurs under divine order. Thus, if our thoughts and actions are Holy, we will bear the "twelve manner of fruits" in the "midst of the garden".

The other well-known, Bible related tree is "The Tree of the Knowledge of Good and Evil." This may be a symbol of ego and free will. If the misguided thought that our lives, intelligence and substance are self-created dominates the mind then the illusion of separation from God will prevail.

The final chapter of this book, in the section on "Exercise," talks about how the Vagus nerve plays an integral part in Sacred Secretion preservation through parasympathetic nerve system dominance.

CHAPTER **21**

Kundalini & Kaya Kalpa

"An amazing activity commences throughout the central nervous system with the awakening of Kundalini -- The body transforms itself into a miniature laboratory, working at high speed day and night -- The innumerable nerve endings extract a nectar like essence from the surrounding tissues, which, travels in two distinct forms; radiation (solar energy) and a subtle essence which streams into the spinal cord (lunar energy)."

Gopi Krishna in "The Biology of Kundalini" by Justin Kerr

For the sake of this book I thought it important to mention how the teachings of Kundalini and the Sacred Secretion are essentially the same paradigm taught via different understandings. Perhaps the differences occur only due to geographical distance and cultural preferences rather than some deliberate mass conspiracy.

Kundalini is an energy represented by two coiled Caduceus serpents, that lay dormant at the base of the spine, until activated and lifted upwards, through the 7 chakras. When the two serpents (matter and antimatter) are lifted upwards they crisscross through the Ida and Pingala Nadis toward the destination of divine unification. Once united the energy creates a bridge between the pineal and pituitary glands. When this transpires, the pineal and pituitary hormones complement one another and the RNA DNA - Immune Hormone Substance (IHS) is transformed through the process of Xenogenesis. There is also an ancient Christogram composed of the letters "IHS", which is an abbreviation for Jesus. This parallel appears to be a genuine coincidence, or perhaps it is a "God-incidence" like the similarity between the name Jesus and the French "Je suis" meaning "I am".

IDA, PINGALA AND SUSHUMNA NADIS

In Sanskrit nadi means flow or vibrational motion. Nadis are energetic pathways throughout the body. There are 72,000 known nadis in the subtle body connecting the chakras. The chakras regulate flow, store energy and distribute energy.

In the Bible Matthew 26:53 (KJV) says, "Thinkest thou that I cannot now pray to my Father, and he shall presently give me more than twelve legions of angels?" There is another striking parallel to be drawn here. A typical Roman legion was 6000 soldiers. Therefore, twelve legions equal 72,000 angels.

The "Pingala Nadi" carries positive solar energy known as "Prana". Prana has an electric quality. The Pingala nadi is connected to the pineal gland.

The "Ida Nadi" carries negative lunar energy known as "Apana". Apana has a magnetic quality. The Ida nadi is connected to the pituitary gland.

These two energies must be combined and balanced in the root chakra before the Kundalini can rise. Through specific breathing techniques and yoga postures the two energies are encouraged to meet in the solar plexus chakra. Here, the two energies coalesce to create a tremendous white heat. The white heat energises the "Sushumna Nadi" which is also known as the silver cord and runs alongside the spinal cord. When the Sushumna is activated it is said to "light up".

The easiest way to understand the Nadis is as the spiritual counterpart of the spinal cord and nerves on either side. The spinal cord and the nerves carry the physical vital fluids from the pineal and pituitary and the nadis carry apana and prana. Thus, they both work together to play the most integral part in the preservation of the Sacred Secretion. As events or emotions occur spiritually within the subtle body, they manifest materially modifying the material body.

> "Otherwise known as the Wand of Hermes, the caduceus
> was a pole with two snakes entwined. The Thyrsus was
> a representation of the caduceus, probably made out of
> a hollow stalk like that of fennel – in which Prometheus
> carried down fire to illumine mankind. The Thyrsus in
> which the secret fire is hidden is the Sushumna Nadi of
> Indian occult physiology."
>
> (Page 264) "The Secret History of the World" by Jonathon Black

Comparable with the central nervous system of our body, the subtle Ida, Pingala and Sushumna nadis show structural similarities between the left and right sympathetic trunks, and the spinal cord respectively - as do the CSF and nerve fluid, the apana and prana show similarities in their flow.

In the caduceus the Ida and Pingala are represented by two serpents criss-crossing in a double helix pattern that intersects at each chakra or energy centre, interestingly this pattern resembles the shape of three "8's" stacked on top of one another; the gematric value of Jesus is of course 888. The Sushumna is shown as a staff. Similar symbolism is used in the Bible when Moses uses his staff to raise the snakes.

The Ida strikes the pituitary, the Pingala strikes the Pineal and the Sushumna strikes the Thalamus. When the Kundalini rises the pineal gland projects radiation towards the pituitary gland and this union unlocks what is known as the "tenth gate" or the crown chakra.

The 3 belt stars in the Orion constellation associated with their respective glands and organ also correspond with the Nadis (see illustration - chapter 31).

KAYA KALPA

The Indian system called "Kaya Kalpa" is sometimes referred to as "Secret Siddha Yoga". Like Kundalini, one of the focuses of Kaya Kalpa is to preserve and transmute sexual energy into spiritual energy. This is achieved mainly through practicing specific breathing techniques and body posturing. Kaya Kalpa is renowned for its ability to rejuvenate the body and even lengthen average human life expectancy.

There are several strands to the Kaya Kalpa system, these include: herbal therapies, breathing techniques and practices, yoga postures and certain dietary guidelines.

The study and practice of Kaya Kalpa Yoga observes and seeks to condition what is described as five corresponding vital bodily systems. These are:

1. The life-force (Divine Energy)
2. The bio-magnetism
3. The sexual vital fluid

4. The mind
5. The physical body

A brief look at the Kaya Kalpa understanding for each of the five will show their importance and correlation to one another:

1. The life-force (Divine Energy) - these are the particles or "substance" that "give life".

2. The bio-magnetism – this is the polar attraction caused by particle rotation that creates a wave and literally holds the body together.

3. The sexual vital fluid – this all-important vital fluid is thought to retain life-force energy. The quantity and quality of sexual vital fluid determines potency and volume of the life-force and bio-magnetism.

4. The mind – approximately 25% of bio-magnetism is utilised by the brain cells enabling us to think, feel, compare, calculate and reflect.

5. The physical body – approximately 75% of bio-magnetism is utilised by the body's metabolic routine including: digestion and the trans-forming of food into flesh, fat, bone, marrow and sexual vital fluid.

This all equates to a practice revolving around the maintaining and hon-ouring of bio-magnetism and sexual vital fluid. It is said that when bio-magnetism becomes weak the cells of the body cannot hold together properly, and this is evidenced as fatigue. Since the sexual vital fluid is what holds the life-force energy it is regarded with the upmost importance.

By increasing the quality and quantity of sexual vital fluid through retention and transmutation, life-force and bio-magnetism intensify thus heightening cell repair and manufacture. Subsequently, all aspects of health and sensory experiences including energy, joy, focus, clarity, memory and adaptability become heightened. Likewise, when the quality and quantity of sexual vital fluid is decreased bodily functions weaken and become impaired. Kaya Kalpa experts say that the study and practice of this ancient teaching can strengthen the body at a cellular level so abundantly that one can avoid all minor and major diseases, as well as living a much longer life than the average western expectancy of 71 years.

CHAPTER 22

Biodynamic Craniosacral Therapy

"thou anointest my head with oil; my cup runneth over."

Psalm 3:5 (KJV)

Biodynamic Craniosacral Therapy was founded by William Garner Sutherland (1873-1954). It is similar to Kundalini yoga which focuses on enhancing the spiritual energy flow within the spine, but instead focuses on enhancing the flow of physical CSF. Craniosacral Therapy is based on the renowned and trusted practise of osteopathy.

Facilitating the body's natural healing processes by restoring the flow of vital fluids, muscle tissues and bones, craniosacral practitioners can help their clients to release pain and restrictive conditions. In order to feel healthy, we need oxygen, blood and nutrients to move freely through our body, creating a better awareness of this will lead to empowerment and self-driven well-being.

Increased CSF flow within the brain creates an environment for altered electrical potentials (gradients) which once again complements and coincides with melatonin enhancements and endogenous DMT production.

"When the supply of cerebrospinal fluid exceeds the volume of the cerebrospinal canal, the ventricles of the brain and the meningeal structures, it seeps out and bathes the nerves, resulting in the experience of an intense sense of physical and spiritual bliss."

(Page 1) [Amrita, Soma, Ambrosia, Nectar, Elixir - Personal Experiences] "The Kundalini Process" by Wim Borsboom

Since Jesus was an enlightened or "Christed" being, he must have known about the mostly disastrous ramifications of drinking alcohol. Therefore, the fact that his first Biblically recorded miracle in the gospel of Mark was the turning of water into wine doesn't quite ring true - unless of course the Scripture was not meant to be taken literally. The symbolic interpretation shows the change and regeneration that takes place within our body, mind and spirit when we nourish ourselves with positive thoughts, actions and emotions. The wine is the new consciousness and it is "better" because the force of spirit (what alcohol is often named after) is activated within the substance at the marriage in Cana (throat). Speaking of wine, the Bible says the following in John 6:56 KJV: "He that eateth my flesh, and drinketh my blood, dwelleth in me, and I in him." Knowing that Jesus' spirit would bring forth purity and remain (dwell) within us.

CHAPTER 23

The Chakras and Nerve Fluid

"The Holy Spirit manifests in humankind through these graces, reflecting the seven spirits of Yahweh. The seven graces are: 1) insight (prophecy); 2) helpfulness (service or ministry); 3) instruction (teaching); 4) encouragement; 5) generosity (giving); 6) guidance (leadership); and 7) compassion."

Romans 12: 6-8 (MSG)

There are 7 prominent energy centres (Chakras) in the human body. The number 7 appears many times in the Bible (and of course the many other sacred texts that predate the Bible) reminding us of the power of these divine energy centres.

The Chakras are centres of activity, which receive, assimilate and transmit divine energy. Each Chakra acts as a gateway reflecting an aspect or influence of consciousness into our lives. Chakras control the flow and distribution of prana or divine energy through the spiritual routes of the Ida, Pingala and Sushumna Nadis and the corresponding physical glands.

Physically speaking this energy is mirrored by the material element of nerve fluid circulating in the 6 major nerve plexuses of the body. It can also be seen Biblically in the "six waterpots of stone" (John 2:6-7 KJV) which are filled with water, or nerve fluid. The reason for there being 7 chakras but only 6 nerve plexuses or "waterpots" is due to the fact that the 6th and 7th chakras are governed by the same nerve plexus, that being the choroid plexus. Every thought sets the nerve fluid into action.

As a quick flowing, universally generative fluid that God propels throughout our bodies the nerve fluid can be likened to "Hiddekel" or "Tigris"; one of the four rivers that flowed out of the Garden of Eden (Genesis 2:14). It is the electro-magnetic centre of every physical atom which enlivens our bodies with the power of divine energy.

The scientific name for nerve fluid is endoneurial fluid and it acts in a similar way to cerebrospinal fluid by forming a blood-nerve barrier. It is the most confined, pressurized and volatile fluid in the body. Many mental and spiritual actions occur because of the flares that take place when the nerve fluid reaches the ends of the nerves.

The six waterpots represent the potential to purify our six nerve plexuses. If this is accomplished the realisation and use of the vibratory power in the voice can become so potent that a "waterpot" full of water can indeed be transmuted into wine.

The 7 Energy Centres (6 nerve plexuses), Seals or Chakras are affected not only by our thoughts, actions, diets and emotions – but also by the rotations and energies of the 7 classic planets. For example, the magnetism of the Root Chakra is reflected in the qualities of Saturn also known as the black sun & Satan.

Both the ancient understandings of the Chakras and the biblical references illustrate the importance of keeping each of the 7 energy centres clear to promote divine physical, mental and spiritual health. Here is an over view of each chakra, its corresponding nerve plexus and other interesting associations.

Chakra One: The Coccygeal/Root Plexus

Biblically known as:

1. The church of Ephesus - "The part of us that has forsaken its true love".

And

2. Sodom, the place that represents the concealed thoughts of man and had to be purified in fire for its few righteous inhabitants to be freed. It was the southernmost city in the vale. We need to fully turn our backs on all forms of carnal desire just like Lot, his wife and his two daughters so that we can know God and fully utilize the Light.

Commonly known as: "The Root Chakra", "The Earth Chakra"
Concerned with: Survival
Expression: "I am"
Blocked By: Fear
Location: Base of spine/coccyx bone
Physical Counterpart: The Gonad Glands (Sexual Glands)
Nerve Plexus: The Coccygeal Plexus is a bundle of nerves situated near the Coccyx Bone.
Element: Earth
Planet: Saturn – ruler of the bones and teeth, ligaments and the mineral salts of the body. Saturn is also known as the planet of lack and deficiency.
Association: Satan
Colour: Red

Shape: Hexahedron

Plane: Physical

Secret Name (Vibration): Lam

When blocked it increases: Laziness, lethargy, loneliness, scepticism and anger.

When flowing it restores: Security, health, vitality.

Chakra Two: The Sacral Plexus

Biblically known as:

1. The Church of Smyrna - "The part of us that suffers persecution".

and

2. Egypt which represents the illusion of mortality. Leaving Egypt means leaving the human consciousness forever and crossing the Red Sea, sacrificing every tie that binds us to the past.

Commonly known as: "The Sacral Plexus", "The Sacrum"

Concerned with: Pleasure

Expression: "I feel"

Blocked by: Guilt

Location: Lower abdomen

Physical Counterpart: The Leyden Gland (digestive and pancreatic)

Nerve Plexus: The Sacral Plexus is a nerve plexus which provides motor and sensory nerves.

Element: Water

Planet: Mars – ruler of the muscular system.

Association: Merodach

Colour: Orange

Shape: Icosahedron

Plane: Astral

Secret Name (Vibration): Vam

When blocked it increases: Feelings of guilt, possessiveness and shame.

When flowing it restores: grace, flexibility, depth of feelings, sexual and creative fulfilment.

Chakra Three: Celiac / Solar Plexus

Biblically known as:

1. The church of Pergamum - "The part of us that needs to repent".

and

2. Bethlehem, which means "house of bread" and is the place where both the historical Jesus and the Christ germ seed are born.

Commonly known as: "The Solar Plexus"

Concerned with: Will power

Expression: "I do"

Blocked by: Shame

Location: Upper Abdomen, Mid-stomach

Physical Counterpart: Adrenal Glands

Nerve Plexus: The Celiac/Coeliac/Solar plexus is a complete network of nerves.

Element: Fire

Colour: Yellow

Planet: Jupiter – ruler of the arterial system, liver and the fats stored in the body.

Association: Bel and Ba'al

Shape: Octahedron

Plane: Mental

Secret Name (Vibration): Ram

When blocked it creates: Self-doubt which can paralyze our ability to take-action due to the assumption of failure, thus causing depression and confusion.

When flowing it restores: Motivation, enthusiasm, harmony and confidence in the knowing that we are continuously being protected.

A microcosmic reflection of the Sun, the solar plexus represents our internal source of energy and personal sense of power. Power incorporates the ability to nurture and create or indeed to destroy. Wisdom is knowing when to nurture and create and when to destroy or rest.

Chakra Four: Cardiac / Heart Plexus

Biblically known as:

1. The Church of Thyatira - "The part of us that has false prophets"

And

2. Jerusalem meaning habitation of peace. In man it is the abiding consciousness of spiritual peace, which is the result of continuous realizations of spiritual power and confidence. Jerusalem is the "city of David," which symbolizes the great nerve centre at the back of the heart. From this point Spirit sends its radiance to all parts of the body.

Commonly known as: "Cardiac Plexus", "Heart Chakra"

Concerned with: Love

Expression: I Love

Blocked by: Grief

Location: Chest, heart, Sternum

Physical Counterpart: Thymus Gland

Nerve Plexus: The Cardiac Plexus is a plexus of nerves that innervates the heart.

Element: Air

Colour: Green

Planet: Venus – ruler of blood, veins, skin and hair.

Association: Hadassah

Shape: Tetrahedron

Plane: Egoic

Secret Name (Vibration): Yam

When blocked it creates: obsessiveness, jealousy and bitterness

When flowing it restores: joy, gratitude and compassion

The Heart Chakra / Cardiac Plexus secretes a powerful peptide hormone (ANF) which affects various regions of the brain including the hypothalamus and pituitary gland.

> "Above all else, guard your heart, for everything
> you do flows from it.
> **Proverbs 4:23 (NIV)**

The operative words here being, "EVERYTHING you do" – reminding us that, due to the persistent and continuous spiritual and physical mechanisms within the body absolutely EVERYTHING we do affects us spiritually and biologically. The natural law of cause and effect means that NOTHING is without consequence. All thoughts and actions count toward success or failure in the preservation of the Sacred Secretion.

Chakra Five: Thyroid / Throat Plexus

Biblically known as:

1. The Church of Sardis - "The part of us that has fallen asleep/ceased to express its truth."

And

2. Bethel situated a few miles north of Jerusalem. Bethel refers to a centre near the heart, which is called the house of God. Jacob thought that it was material, when he lay down there with a stone for a pillow; but he found there a ladder reaching to heaven, and he exclaimed: "Surely God is in this place; and I knew it not". Beth-el symbolizes a consciousness of God, or conscious unity with God.

Commonly known as: "Throat Chakra"
Concerned with: Truth
Expression: I speak
Blocked by: The lies that we tell ourselves and the deceptions that we choose to believe
Location: Throat
Physical Counterpart: The Thyroid Gland
Nerve Plexus: The Pharyngeal plexus is a network of nerves innervating most of the palate and pharynx.

Element: Sound

Colour: Light Blue

Planet: Mercury – ruler of the brain and nervous system and has a determining effect on the electromagnetic vibrations of the body.

Association: Hermes

Shape: Dodecahedron

Plane: Intuitive

Secret Name (Vibration): Ham

When blocked it creates: an inability to express ourselves, defend ourselves and say no to others.

When flowing it restores: the ability to express our truth without worrying and diplomatically share our opinion with kindness, courage and conviction.

Chakra Six: Pituitary / Brow Plexus

Biblically known as:

1. The Church of Philadelphia - "The part of us that has endured patiently."

And

2. Haran meaning strong, elevated and exalted or mountain. It was here that Terah, Abraham's father, died (Gen. 11:32). An exalted state of mind, wherein truth is revealed in consciousness and the individual is strengthened in his determination to go on toward fuller spiritual enlightenment.

Commonly known as: "The Mind Chakra"

Concerned with: Insight

Expression: "I see"

Blocked by: Illusion

Location: Forehead, between the eyebrows.

Physical Counterpart: Pituitary Gland

Nerve Plexus: Choroid Plexus (l)

Element: Light

Planet: Moon – ruler of magnetism and influencer of the medulla oblongata where magnetism is stored.

Association: Jaroah

Colour: Blue

Shape: Sphere

Plane: Casual

Secret Name (Vibration): Sham

When blocked it creates: denial, irritability and distrust.

When flowing it restores: enthusiasm, the realization of our divinity and an innate sense of knowingness - all illusions will disappear.

Chakra Seven: Pineal / Crown Plexus

Biblically known as:

1. The Church of Laodicea - "The part of us that is lukewarm or insipid to God".

And

2. Peniel - the place where Jacob met God face to face.

Commonly known as: "The Crown Chakra"

Concerned with: Thought

Expression: I understand

Blocked by: Attachments to earthly "things" and "beliefs"

Location: Top or crown of the head

Physical Counterpart: Pineal Gland

Nerve Plexus: Choroid Plexus (ll)

Element: Cosmic

Colour: Purple

Planet: Sun – ruler of vitality and energy stored in the spleen.

Association: Jesus

Shape: Star Tetrahedron

Plane: Spiritual

Secret Name (Vibration): Aum/Om

When blocked it creates: a fixation with people and things that have conditioned us to think within the borders of the visual human realm.

When flowing it restores: supernatural sight, visions from God and confidence in our own God-given intuition.

CHAPTER 24

Sacrum & Sacral Pump

"When the Kundalini, the serpent fire that lies concealed within the sacral plexus is awakened, burns up the dross within the spinal cord, and reaches the conarium (another name for the pineal gland), it sets fire to this oil and thus lights the perpetual lamp."

Page 110 "God-Man: The World Made Flesh" By George W. Carey and Ines Eudora Perry

The Sacral Pump is a regular rhythmic motion between the "Occiput" and the sacrum near the base of the spine. It circulates CSF back up the spinal cord and into the brain. The sacral pump is a key part of the circulatory system and its proper functioning is important for good physical, mental and emotional well-being.

The Sacrum is a triangular bone in the lower back formed from five fused vertebrae and situated between the two hip bones of the pelvis. The English word "sacrum" was introduced as a technical term in anatomy in the mid-18th century, as a shortening of the late Latin name *os sacrum* «sacred bone». It is the region near where surgeons perform a lumbar puncture to extract samples of CSF and is the location of the "Sacral Pump".

Biblically, five stands for sacrifice and the five tangible senses. There are: 5 foolish virgins, 5 wise virgins, 5 wounds of Jesus, David picked 5 stones to kill Goliath; although he only used one and there are five Kings in the book of Joshua - which some say is actually the book of Jesus.

When Israel entered the Promised Land there were five kings with armies who were determined to stop them. Lovingly, God helped Joshua to defeat them and the kings ran to hide in a cave. Joshua then ordered his soldiers to bring each king out one by one. Each king was then put to death by having his neck stood on!

Each king represents one of the five senses: seeing, hearing, smelling, tasting and touching. God does not want us to live according to their dictates. Our senses are susceptible to every outward experience; positive and negative. But faith gives us hope, power and most importantly vision. The act of standing on the king's necks shows how we must put our foot down and take authority over material illusions such as fear and lack. The "demons" or destructive states of consciousness described in chapter 19 are always present, ready to "kill, steal and destroy" (John 10:10). These "demons" work most effectively via the five senses, making dangers and disappointments appear terrifying and disabling. 2 Corinthians 5:7 says that we must "walk by faith and not by sight". Faith says, "In spite of what I feel, regardless of what I hear, see, taste and smell everything is going to be alright because God is with me and the Holy Spirit is within me." Our five senses can be faith-killers and dream-stealers unless we make a stand and put them firmly under our foot.

Below the 5 sacral vertebrae that correspond to our senses are the 4 vertebrae of the coccyx that correspond to the four-fold nature of the psyche: physical, intellectual, spiritual and emotional. The 5 + the 4 = 9 (The number of Divinity).

CHAPTER **25**

Medulla Oblongata

"It is in this way that I have recognized that the prime motive power of respiration has its seat in the medulla oblongata"

"Nineteenth Century Origins of Neuroscientific Concepts" by Julien Jean César Legallois

The Medulla oblongata is located in the brain stem at the base of the brain and the top of the spinal cord. It is the entry and exit point for vital fluids from the brain to the body and vice versa.

The Medulla contains the cardiac, respiratory, vomiting and vasomotor centres and therefore deals with the autonomic functions of breathing, heart rate and blood pressure; all of which are vital for the circulation of CSF.

The roots of the vagus nerve are in the medulla oblongata, at the base of the small brain or cerebellum explaining why death follows the severing of the medulla. It controls the heart action, and if a drug such as aconite be administered, even in small doses, its effect upon this nerve is shown in slowing the action of the heart and decreasing the blood pressure. In larger doses it paralyzes the ends of the vagus in the heart so that the pulse becomes suddenly very rapid and at the same time irregular.

In his book, "The Twelve Powers of Man" Charles Fillmore explains how each of the "mind faculties" in man are symbolized by one of the twelve disciples of Jesus. Here are his proposed character, faculty and body position correlations:

1. John – Love – Heart
2. Matthew – Will – Centre of brain
3. Peter – Faith – The pineal gland
4. Philip – Power – Root of the tongue
5. James (son of Zebedee) – Judgement - Lower stomach
6. James (son of Alphaeus) -- Navel
7. Andrew – Strength – Lower back
8. Judas – Self Preservation – Genitals
9. Thaddaeus – Surrender – Lower back
10. Bartholomew / Nathanael – Imagination – Between the eyes
11. Thomas – Understanding – Front brain
12. Simon – Zeal (Determination) – Medulla

Isn't it interesting to see how Fillmore pinpointed "zeal" in the Medulla? Simon represents the fact that zeal for an idea, or determination to accomplish a goal encourages vital fluid into the medulla. In the medulla the fluid is infused with air and flared through to the pineal, where it is ignited and flashes into light. In other words, when Spirit meets the vital fluid in the medulla at the throat chakra a transmutation, refining or crucifixion occurs right before the whole body is filled with a "finer essence". The medulla literally diffuses vital fluids and distributes them to the senses. Thus, it manifests our thoughts and emotions into perceivable "feelings".

CHAPTER 26

Male and Female

"The twin souls, male and female, or heavenly Osiris and
Isis (father and mother) form two halves, the masculine
and feminine attributes of the divine ego."

(Page 23) [The Origin of Physical Life] "The Light of Egypt" by
Thomas H. Burgoyne

God or Divine Energy is undivided. God is pure creative Love and
Light. But in order to become manifest on the physical plane God
must divide and become the two halves that we see, feel and experience
within ourselves and the universe: male and female, electric and magnetic,
sun and moon, pineal and pituitary secretions, solar secretion (solar rays)
and lunar seeds (moon energy), Ida and Pingala etc. Furthermore, this
is scientifically reflected in the study of "magnetic reconnection," - a
process that occurs in conductive plasmas (such as CSF, nerve fluid and
blood). Magnetic topology is rearranged and converted into kinetic
energy, thermal energy and particle acceleration.

Since our thoughts and emotions bring "things" into being, the
importance of harmonising the duality within ourselves is paramount for
the progression of unconditional love and limitless power both internally

creating health, joy and bliss and externally creating a catalyst toward peace, healing and unity across the Earth. The process of reuniting the Divine energy within ourselves by dissolving fear and upgrading our secretions makes each human the embodiment of "the word (seed) made flesh" just as Jesus was. The "Word is God" means that the "seed is God" and the seed is the Divine Energy that creates EVERYTHING.

The "seed" flows down from heaven where it is received by the claustrum and divided by the physical pineal and the pituitary and the ethereal Ida and Pingala before descending and ascending through the spinal cord and the Sushumna.

> "The Kabbalistic initiates, of the ages that are gone, formulated this same biune spirit as love (female) and wisdom (male). Love as the negative or feminine ray, is content and ever seeks to enfold. Wisdom as the positive, masculine ray, is restless and always in pursuit."
>
> (Page 29) [The Mysteries of Sex] "The Light of Egypt" by Thomas H. Burgoyne

The verb root "or" within "word" and "lord", means living-light or Gold. The "O" is male, and the "R" is female; together they are the "Or" which is the divine golden "substance" and highlights the divine union once more.

A few more examples:

Frankincense (Male) and Myrrh (Female) = Gold (God)

Honey from the Pineal (Male) and Milk from the Pituitary (Female) = The Chemical Wedding

Moses is Jachin (Male) and Aaron is Boaz (Female) = Two Pillars

Solar Energy (Masculine) and Lunar Energy (Feminine) = The Divine Luni-Solar

An atom of hydrogen (Masculine) unites with an atom of carbon (Feminine) = Solar Light

The space in between the Pineal and the Pituitary is called the "Crystal Palace" by Daoists and is the birth place of the physical "I am" experience. Through dispersion of the energy within the CSF, the entire brain is bathed in differentiated energy from God which creates a synchronous experience of "I am" or "Christ Consciousness."

CHAPTER 27

The Sun

"With Christ, darkness cannot succeed. Darkness will not gain victory over the light of Christ."

"The Hope of God's Light" [General conference for the church of the latter-day saints April 2013] President Dieter F. Uchtdorf

Associations: Spirit, Gold (father of all metals), the crude matter of the sun is Sulphur, the red elixir of sexual alchemy that transforms lead into Gold, the pineal gland, the 7th Chakra or Crown Chakra.

The Sun gives us life and warmth, but it also gives to our Spirit. The ancient's belief is that behind the physical sun which you see in the heavens is a spiritual radiation, the spiritual life-force which feeds and sustains all life on earth. The Spiritual Sun is the "light of lights", it creates unity and synthesis. It is this spiritual counterpart of the Sun which those in the spirit world worship as the "cosmic Christ". But the cosmic Christ is not only a radiation, powerful unseen and too often unfelt: it has a form, a human form. Not confined to one human, but a great power that can manifest through a perfectly beautiful human form. There are many references to Sun worship in the Bible, but they are not recognised as such – there is Sun worship on the outer plane, and there is the Sun of the inner plane, hidden within the teachings of Christ. How can we recognise and understand the true Christ-Sun worship, as apart from what scholars describe as "pagan religion"? True Christ-Sun worship becomes known when a person is vivified by the power of the Spirit in his or her own heart. Anyone can accumulate knowledge, but until the "Son" within becomes ablaze it will not get them very far. The Sun that the ancients worshipped was not so much the physical Sun, but the Spirit that it represented; the loving light, the warm comforter, the provider of life, the patient enduring giver. The sun represents the glorious Christ Spirit within man, the light within our hearts that loves to rise just as the Sun rises each day. This is the ultimate life, the growth of "Son" qualities within our hearts making us true people of God.

CHAPTER 28

The Moon

"when (the moon is) configurated with other orbs; her influx becomes exceedingly potent as she receives and transmits to us the intensified influence of those stars aspecting her."

(Page 260) "The Light of Egypt" by Thomas H. Burgoyne

Associations: Soul, Silver (mother of all metals), the crude matter of the moon is Mercury, the white elixir of sexual alchemy that purifies and whitens the base metals (Lead), the pituitary gland, the 6th Chakra or Brow Chakra.

As the moon moves through alignment with the sun signs, spending approximately 2.5 days in each, it magnifies and transmits the energetic influence of the stars in that particular constellation toward earth and into our bodies. Therefore, when the moon is aligned with an individual person's sun sign the influx of their divine energy becomes exceedingly potent.

"The Prāna, or breath of the human organism, is a part
of this universal vital principle. The moon also is shown
to have its share in nourishing all organic matter, and in
regulating the ebb and flow of the Prāna of nature. With
every phase of the moon the Prāna of man changes its
course."

(Page 28) "Monism or Advaitism?" By Manilal Nabhubhai Dvivedi

The planet Earth which we live upon absorbs an energy that we as humans
at this point in history cannot by nature or science fully understand or
appreciate. We only receive this energy as an astral influx by the reflective
action of our Earth's satellite, the Moon. This influence is neither good
nor evil; it is an amalgamation of stellar, planetary and solar energies all
stemming from God the source. As will be explained in subsequent chapters, the composition of this "astral influx" changes according to stellar,
planetary, solar and lunar positions. It is the differentiations within this
energy that creates the wonderful characteristics, talents, interests and
idiosyncrasies of each individual "self". When the moon travels through
the same position that it was in at the time of a person's birth, the "astral
influx" will contain the same influences, or energies that were presented
to us or installed into us from or by God through the atmosphere at the
time of birth. Therefore, optimising our abilities and helping us know
ourselves far more clearly.

For further information about lunar influence I recommend reading
the essays and articles available on www.tandfonline.com under "moon
influence".

In reference to the crude matter of the moon being "mercury"; a
very prominent factor in mystical alchemy, it is interesting to observe a

parallel. Mercury (Hg) is naturally present in coal (what Santa gives us if we are naughty) and still remains in its ashes after combustion. Again, this illustrates the transforming energy and material composites of divine spirit within the body,

"He makes beauty out of ashes"

Isaiah 61:3 (KJV)

The metallic element of mercury is also known as quicksilver; "quick" in the sense of "living".

The Latin term for torture is crucifixion or "cruciatus" and includes anything from flogging to strangulation. The crucifixion of Mercury is any severe treatment that causes it to change form (or upgrade it from coal). In "Le Tractatus parabolicus du pseudo-Arnaud de Villeneuve" by Antoine Calvet there is a detailed comparison between the transformation of Mercury and the torments of Jesus.

I considered including a chapter on each of the planets within this analysis, but there is a plethora of books and online sources already available. I do believe however that Mercury deserves a brief mention in relation to the "Christ". Astrologers know that Mercury holds an important position in our lives. Mercury represents the mind and is linked to the illuminating principle of human life. The planet Mercury emanates energies of what is known as the "Fourth Ray" of the "Seven Universal Rays" and as such, it is connected with the function of human intelligence that separates mankind from the animal kingdom.

Mind allows humanity to be a conscious vessel for the streaming of energies from planetary and celestial influences. In this sense, Mercury is the messenger of the gods. In terms of mysticism Mercury is an esoteric symbol for "Word" as in "Lost Word"; the pagan god Mercury is a "messenger" delivering "Words".

Mercury is associated with duality and all facets of communication. It plays a vital role in two other areas of relatedness; it synthesises our thoughts and experiences into wisdom, thus assisting the distribution of the "Second Ray" (Love and Wisdom). This facilitates the evolutionary and regressive currents that condition the relationship between the Soul and the personality.

CHAPTER 29

The Stars (Sun Signs)

"That energy is God's energy, an energy deep within you, God himself willing and working at what will give him the most pleasure. Do everything readily and cheerfully - no bickering, no second-guessing allowed! Go out into the world uncorrupted, a breath of fresh air in this squalid and polluted society. Provide people with a glimpse of good living and of the living God. Carry the light-giving Message into the night."

Philippians 2:13-15 (MSG)

Consisting of luminous spheroid plasma, stars are a type of astronomical object. Historically the most prominent stars were grouped into constellations and given the names that we now know as the 12 signs of the zodiac or star/sun signs.

Stars shine due to the thermonuclear fusion of hydrogen and helium in their core, releasing energy that radiates into space and is transmitted to Earth.

ALMOST every naturally occurring element heavier than helium is created by the stars (stellar nucleosynthesis) and stars are born or come into existence in stellar nurseries such as the Orion Nebula.

Every day (24 hours period) the sun moves through each of these 12 sun signs, spending 2 hours in each and each one is related to a different part of the body. I recommend reading "Relation of the Mineral Salts of the Body to the Signs of the Zodiac" by George W. Carey if this is a subject that intrigues you.

Every Luni-Solar month (Approximately 29.53 days) the sun moves through each of these 12 sun signs, spending approximately 2.5 days in each.

Those of us who have been influenced by the "church" will know that 10% of income is the recommended amount of money to give or tithe. This percentage comes from the word "tithe" itself, meaning "tenth":

> "A tithe (/taɪð/; from Old English: teogoþa "tenth") is a
> one-tenth part of something"
> Dictionary.com

But tithing did not originally pertain to money, rather the true tithe was 10% of the 29.53-day synodic month, i.e. the 2.5 days that the moon is in the individual's birth or sun sign. The offering should be of ourselves to God. Tithing our 10% conscious mind, all carnal thoughts, actions and desires and totally surrendering ourselves to God in a disposition of unconditional love or Bhakti through prayer (talking to God), meditation (listening to God), worship (giving thanks) and yoga or another form of exercise that engages the breath to condition the temple during those days is how God then gives us access to the 90% subconscious mind. The "first fruits" are our first thoughts, first attention, first love, first gratitude on the first days of our personal monthly cycle and they should be 100% sacrificed to knowing and loving God.

> "Any act, coming under the meaning of sin, retards or prevents the automatic action of the seed, which, if not interfered with, lifts up a portion (one-tenth) of the life essence (oil or secretion) that constantly flows down the spinal cord (a "straight and narrow way") and transmutes it, thus increasing its power many fold and perpetuating the body indefinitely, or until the Ego desires to dissolve it by rates of motion set in action by its inherent will."
>
> (Page 21) "God-Man: The Word Made Flesh" by George W. Carey and Ines Eudora Perry

This does not mean that giving to your church or anyone else will not reap the rewards put forth by many doctrines because, the laws of nature work in the macrocosm as well as the microcosm. Giving on any level cannot be a bad thing, especially when done with a true and generous Spirit and not a desire to "get back". Giving is a form of surrender; sharing spreads love, hope, joy and faithfulness and the law of nature that says, "what we sow we shall reap" or "what goes around comes around" is an undeniable fact. Besides this, being stingy, possessive, not repaying debts and or concealing wealth essentially shows a lack of faith and trust in abundance from God. This attitude creates a very low vibratory frequency and basically says, "I am betting against God's abilities to bless me". We will never know the majestic extent of Gods blessings if we are too busy trying to bless ourselves.

CHAPTER 30

The Timing

"There is one glory of the sun, and another glory
of the moon, and another glory of the stars: for
one star differeth from another star in glory."

1 Corinthians 15:41 (KJV)

Speaking in terms of the macrocosm and the microcosm, it's important to visualise the correct associations between the human microcosm and the universal macrocosm:

The Astrological Constellations (Star/Sun Signs: Aries, Taurus, Gemini, Cancer, Leo, Virgo, Libra, Scorpio, Sagittarius, Capricorn, Aquarius and Pisces) = The body

The Moon = The Soul

The Sun = The Spirit

Saturn, Jupiter, Mars, Venus, and Mercury = The Five Physical Senses (Biblically: 5 kings that were to be put to death by having their necks stood on)

It is this connection that leaves us susceptible to various combinations of subtle energetic planetary influences. In Quantum physics, the "Implicate Order" of physicist David Bohm proposes that the physical, psychic and spiritual realms are ultimately connected. Evidence for this hypothesis can be found in the scientific study of bioelectrical and biochemical processes:

> "The idea of the coupling of the bioelectrical and biochemical process in the human organism is alien to the classical research on the psychological life. This new approach postulates a holistic account of the human being and his environment. The model, in referring to psychology, is very inspiring, because it postulates the reception of information from the environment not only via sense receptors, but also through the entire mass of the biological organism, understood as organic piezoelectric, pyroelectric and semiconductors."
>
> NeuroQuantology (December 2011, Vol 9, Issue 4, Page 681-691) "Bio-plasma Concept of Consciousness" by Adam Grzegorz Adamski

Plutarch said that: "The divine spirit is to the soul what the soul is to the body." This means that in the same way that the sun reflects light off of the moon down to earth, the spirit shines light into our body via the soul.

The moon's energy is magnetic, and the sun's energy is electric. Together they are the electromagnetic female (moon) and male (sun). They are the essence of all forms.

The sacred Luni-Solar calendar is used in many cultures including Hebrew, Buddhist, Hindu, Chinese, Tibetan and Korean. The Luni-Solar calendar incorporates the phase of the moon, as well as the time of the solar year.

> "This Naros is the Luni-Solar Naros, or Sibylline year. It is composed of 31 periods of 19 years and one of 11, and is the most perfect of astronomical cycles, and, although no chronologer has mentioned it at length, it is the most ancient of all. It consists of 600 years, or 7200 Solar months, or 219,146.5 days, and this same number of days, 219,146.5, gives 600 years consisting of 365 days, 5 hours, 51 minutes and 36 seconds, which differs less than 3 minutes from what the length is observed to be this day."
>
> (Page 123) [Naronia] "Light of Egypt" by Thomas H. Burgoyne

1 Naronian year, also known as a Sibylline year or 1 Messianic Cycle is the same length as one full Luni-Solar cycle which is approximately 600 years or 7200 Solar months. The Synodic period of the moon (including the Sidereal period / 2.5-day time delta), is 29.53 days long. That is the amount of time it takes the moon to travel through all 12 sun signs.

> "This cycle is the most inviolable of all. It was repeated in symbolic figures only in the Chaldean book of numbers, the original book, which, if now extant is not to be found in libraries."
>
> (Vol.1, Pages 31-33) "Isis Unveiled" by Madam Blavatsky

Looking at this "inviolable"; meaning, not to be altered or infringed, cycle more closely is what gives us the dates for our individual Sacred Secretion processes because the Creator's (God's) original calendar was indeed a Luni-Solar Calendar.

According to Leviticus 23:1-4 God wanted us to celebrate his "feast" days and the moon and sun were placed in order for us to know when these feast days are.

> "And God said, Let there be lights in the firma-
> ment of the heaven to divide the day from the
> night; and let them be for signs, and for seasons,
> and for days, and years"
>
> **Genesis 1:14 (KJV)**

The book of Genesis also says that the "day" begins at sunset (Genesis 1:5 KJV) and that each month starts on the day of the "New Moon" (Numbers 10:10 and Psalm 81:3 KJV). The etymological study of the word "month" shows that the Hebrew word "Chodesh", the Aramaic word "yerach" and the Greek word "men" all derive from the word "moon" which means, "a division of the year derived from the period required by the moon to pass through four phases, as from one new moon to the next". The New Moon is the first appearance of a slither of the moon after it's been completely dark or seemingly invisible for a few days. In Exodus 12:2 (KJV) God told Moses that the year should begin in spring, this first month was known as "Abib" and began after the spring equinox (approximately 18-22nd March). Two weeks or fourteen days after the spring equinox is the correct time for the Passover. Six new moons or "months" later, on the first day of the seventh month is the Feast of

Trumpets or autumn equinox (approximately 18-22nd September). There are more "feasts" listed in Leviticus, all of which correspond with the "lights in the firmament".

Today's months are merely artificial, man-made periods that conveniently distract us from the ancient practice of observing the phases of the moon in relation to the sun and stellar constellations that God put in the sky for us.

The Moon-Void is the period of time when the moon stops aspecting or aligning to other planets in one sun sign while it moves into the next. Due to the Moon-Void, the correct time to start the process of Sacred Secretion preservation is approximately 12-24 hours BEFORE the moon enters your individual sun sign (the zodiacal sign that you were born under). It is useful to observe this void period because if the Divine energy penetrates an unprepared vessel (human organism) it will instantly be diluted upon arrival.

But, should this be calculated using the tropical system or the Sidereal system?

You may be familiar with these two main systems; tropical and sidereal. So, which one is "correct"? Research shows that in fact both systems correspond to one another and both are used in biodynamic agriculture.

The Tropical Zodiac is the position of the sun referenced against the earth's horizon. The Sidereal Zodiac is the position of the sun referenced against the stars. Arguably, the Sidereal (Vedic) system is more accurate than the tropical system calculated by the seasons. This is because the sidereal system allows for the fact that not all of the constellations are the same size. However, the tropical system does coincide directly with the equinoxes and also offers a compelling set of reasons for the accuracy of its results.

So, can both Zodiacal systems be compared against one another?

Yes, when represented as wheels they can be superimposed to make one comprehensive calculator. To align the two systems the sun can be used as a common point. By comparing the two wheels a difference of around 25 degrees is found between them. Over time it has been realized that the difference is gradually increasing and that the seasons are slowly moving in relation to the star background by one degree every 70 odd years. This is known as the "Precession of the Equinoxes".

A beautiful part of "The God Design" is revealed through the comparison of these two systems... namely, the simple and marvellous fact that the heavenly zodiac (sidereal) is actually reflected or imprinted onto the earth - giving us the tropical zodiac! This is why BOTH systems are used in Biodynamic Agriculture.

Due to the correspondence of these two systems it is difficult to know which one to use when honouring and preserving the Sacred Secretion. Further evidence reveals an interesting quote from George W. Carey in the book "GOD-MAN: The Word Made Flesh":

> "The date that they made the sun enter Aries was March 21st. Why? March 21st should be the first day of Aries, the head; April 19th should be the first day of Taurus, the neck, and so on through the twelve signs; but these designing schemers knew that by thus supressing the truth the people might come to realise what was meant by "the heavens declare the glory of God."
>
> Again: the moon, in its monthly round of 29.5 days enters the outer stars (or suns) of a constellation two and one half days before it enters the central suns of the

constellations that are known as the signs of the zodiac or the "circle of beasts" (Biblically – Mazzaroth).

But even unto this day the whole anti-Christ world except the astrologers, go by almanac (tropical system) that make the moon enter a sign of the zodiac two- and one-half days before it does enter it and thus perpetuates the lie of the pagan Constantine, the anti-Christ."

Page 92 [The Anti-Christ]

This quote is compellingly backed up by the fact that the Tropical system is more or less two- and one-half days ahead of the Sidereal system. Although I personally find the tone a little harsh and assumptive due to the fact that the difference between the two systems all boils down to a simple matter of space, distance and perspective.

If you prefer to be meticulous in your own planning and practice, there are Apps available like:

"Stellarium" this shows a view of the actual stars via an intuitive satellite system
And
"Deluxe Moon" which allows you to switch between two modes: Tropical and Sidereal

For reasons discussed here, I personally prefer to observe both the Tropical AND Sidereal calendars, although I instinctively believe that the Sidereal system is optimal. An easy way to remember it if you're using a tropical calendar is that the sidereal times are approximately 2.5 days after the tropical times. I recommend looking at the information available at www.astro-calendar.com which explains clearly and in depth the importance of both the tropical and the sidereal systems. As technology, research and consciousness progresses I am sure that these times will be a lot easier to calculate, recognise and honour.

> "More depends upon the position, aspect and power of the sun and moon at birth, than upon all the planets in the solar system combined. For this reason, the SUN AND MOON ARE, TO US, THE TRANSMITTERS OF THE STELLAR FORCES. They act in the capacity of astral mediums and cast their gathered or reflected potencies into our magnetic atmosphere, harmoniously or discordantly, according as they are aspected by the benefic or malefic rays of the major planets. The only difference between the two being, the SUN IS ELECTRIC IN ITS ACTION, HENCE POSITIVE; and the MOON IS MAGNETIC AND NEGATIVE. In themselves alone they are neither fortunate nor unfortunate"
>
> (Page 206) "The Light of Egypt" by Thomas H. Burgoyne

Applying this explanation to the body we see an internal reflection analogous to that occurring between the moon and the sun. With no light of its own, the moon reflects the light of the sun down to earth. Within the human brain this is paralleled by the pineal gland which represents the sun, and the "moon gland", which can modify and reflect is the pituitary gland.

Take for example the ebb and flow of ocean tides. When the earth, sun and moon all line up at the full or new moons we get the extreme "spring tides" – the highest high and lowest low tides. It is the same upon the mental plane within the human brain. The brain magnetically expands and becomes illuminated by the influx of Luni-Solar energy.

> "When the Moon, in the course of her motion, arrives at the same point place during each month, she impregnates these seeds and endows them with magnetic life; therefore, in an occult sense, she confers upon humanity the powers and possibilities of magical forces. It is this Luni-Solar influx of Naronia within the human constitution, then, that controls the real foundation and basis of spiritual development and occult power."
>
> (Page 126) [Naronia] "Light of Egypt" by Thomas H. Burgoyne

To summarise:

According to occult science, distant stars as well as our local Sun (which is also a star) emanate an invisible stellar influence which acts in a subtle way, similar to the proposed physical mechanism (panspermia) for seeding the building blocks of biological life throughout the universe. The stellar influence that we receive from our Sun are the "solar seeds" described by occult science. The combined energies of distant planets, stars and our nearby Sun are what the moon reflects into our human organism. "IT" (the divine energy of planets, stars, sun and moon) comes into our bodies as one but upon arrival must divide in order to manifest materially. It is the preserving of this Sacred Secretion that gives them the opportunity to reunite thus allowing them to fructify within us.

"While travelling the heavens and crossing the zodiac constellation after constellation, the Moon is charging itself with the power and qualities of the currently visited zodiac sign."

www.lunaf.com

CHAPTER 31

The Resurrection

"when Jesus prophesied that the Temple would be rebuilt
in three days, he of course meant his own body"

(Page 561) "The Secret History of the World" by Jonathan Black

According to the "The Metaphysical Dictionary" at www.truthunity. com the metaphysical meaning of "tomb" is "resting place". Joseph of Arimathea insisted that Jesus Christ's body was allowed to be placed in one of his tombs, despite the fact that Jesus did not meet the criteria given by the state to deserve such a tomb. Therefore, Joseph can be seen to represent wise choices and a higher sense of consciousness. The "seed" of truth within Jesus did not die but was gradually spreading and preparing for the final test: the overcoming of the appearance of death.

Similar to the 3 days that Jesus spent in the tomb, the time that we spend resting and honouring God improves our character and therefore our biology along all lines. Not only does our understanding and perceptive consciousness increase and mature, but the "substance" gathers strength and vitality ready for the day of the glorious resurrection. According to the Bible, the manifestation of this process can express itself in varying degrees. This goes a long way to explain the differences between the testimonies of those who have experienced this enlightenment.

> "But he that received seed into the good ground is he
> that heareth the word, and understandeth it; which also
> beareth fruit, and bringeth forth, some an hundredfold,
> some sixty, some thirty."
>
> Matthew 13:23 (KJV)

It's no wonder then that awe, shock and humility fell upon those who witnessed this enlightenment for they would have seen the power and glory become manifest.

> "And after three days and an half the spirit of life from
> God entered into them, and they stood upon their feet;
> and great fear fell upon them which saw them."
>
> Revelation 11:11 (KJV)

The two counterparts of the Resurrection go hand in hand. As previously mentioned, one cannot operate without the other. They are spiritual and physical and are seen Biblically as: Jerusalem (Spiritual) and Jericho (Physical).

SPIRITUAL:

The spiritual resurrection happens when the extroverted, electrical, solar energy in the Pingala nadi and the introverted, magnetic, lunar energy in the Ida nadi reunite and rise to the thalamus as one.

PHYSICAL:

The physical parallel of the resurrection happens when the pineal and pituitary secretions synchronise. The pituitary chemicals of oxytocin and vasopressin, created by a high vibratory frequency of unconditional love, allow CSF flow to increase and pressurize so that the pineal can upgrade melatonin.

This two-fold process encourages blood cell production and dormant brain cell activation. The ancients called anyone who had this experience a "Christ" (Anointed one).

> "When the oil (ointment) is crucified (increased in power a thousand-fold) it remains two and a half days in the tomb and on the third day ascends to the Pineal Gland that connects the cerebellum with the optic thalamus, the central eye in the throne of God."
>
> (Page 90) "God-Man the Word Made Flesh" by George W. Carey and Ines Eudora Perry

The following illustration offers a summary of all that is explored and analysed within this book. I created it myself in order to assist a holistic understanding and visualisation of the combined information. This illustration is simply an expression. It is NOT to scale and nor are the positions of things proportionate or precise. I am not suggesting that any-thing not included in this illustration is of less importance. Divine energy is everywhere, not in just one strand as shown here. I have expressed it this way for the sake of simplicity.

The Holy Temple Body is "fearfully and wonderfully made," EVERY inch of its design and structure - both internally and externally is glorious and worth honouring.

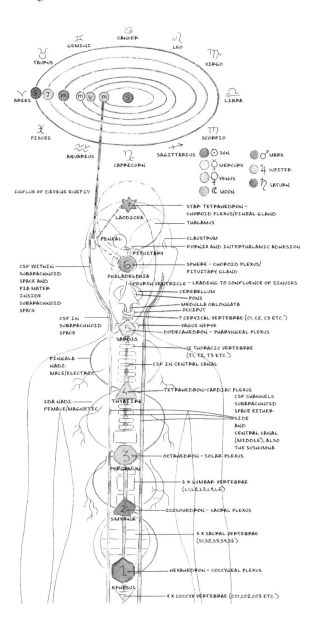

CHAPTER 32

End Times & Prophecy

At this time in history it can be seen that a mass awakening did indeed initiate some time ago or at least, that the gradual evolution of human consciousness has made it appear that way. This glorious, mind-altering, consciousness-raising awakening continues to expand at an undeniable pace. Thus, meaning that the following prophecy could indeed be manifesting as I write:

"At the end of the year 1880, the great archangel Michael (The Sun – The Kingdom – The Power) comes into power and once more has the government of the world until the year AD 2188. This will be a period of imperial greatness. Empires will shine full of glory, the human intellect will have full play and all churches, Religious creeds and Ecclesiastical Dogmas will fall to the ground and become things of the past. Parsons, Vicars and Bishops will have to work in different fields if they mean to obtain an honest livelihood. Yes, I repeat this prophecy. The churches and chapels will fall with a terrible crash and be destroyed. But from their ashes, Phoenix-like, shall arise a new religion, whose shining motto will be; Veritas Excelsior, TRUTH ABOVE."

(Page 115) [La Clef] "The Light of Egypt" by Thomas H. Burgoyne

I have asked John R Francis to write the rest of this chapter on my behalf. John is the author of a wonderful book titled, "The Mystic Way of Radiant Love: Alchemy for a New Creation". John kindly offered to proofread this book that you are reading and subsequently wrote the Foreword and two appendices for it. The reason I have asked him to write this chapter is because although I knew in my spirit that God wanted me to include it, I felt that John's expertise in this area far outweighed my own. Over to John:

A strictly literal interpretation of the Bible might lead one to believe that the world will soon end, and Jesus will physically descend to Earth out of the clouds to assume a kingly throne and rule Earth. However, a metaphorical, mystical interpretation of what appear to be literal prophecies in the Bible will reveal a very different vision for the future but one no less hopeful and exciting.

The belief that the world will end soon comes in part from a mistranslation of the word "eon" found in Greek manuscripts of the New Testament. An "eon" in Greek means a finite duration of time or an "age" – and not the world. The earth has passed through a number of historical and geological ages in the past and is still here now. It will continue to exist physically after humanity transitions out of this current spiritually "dark" age.

For example, when we read in the Bible (KJV) Jesus saying, "so shall it be at the end of the world" (Matthew 13:49), according to the authoritative "Strong's Bible Concordance," the word translated as "world" is actually eon (aion) - which means an age.

However, if one reads the writings of Saint Paul in the Bible (KJV) there are a number of passages where this same Greek word "eon" has been correctly translated as an "age." For example, we read: "the ages to come" (Ephesians 2:7, KJV) and "even the mystery which hath been hidden from ages... but is now made manifest to his saints." (Colossians 1:26, KJV). That mystery being revealed to Christ's followers is: "Christ in you, the hope of glory" (Colossians 1:27).

Notice in that last quote from Paul that the mystery being revealed is the inner presence of Christ that had been hidden from humanity in previous ages. Thus, the outward appearance of Christ physically to his disciples was to awaken them to the inner presence of Christ that had always been there but hidden and suppressed for ages. This was done by literal-minded religious "authorities" by keeping people's attention focused on external rituals, rules and dogmas and away from inner communion with the Christ within.

This validates the main theme of this book regarding the inner presence of Christ. It also explains why the mystical understanding of End Times Prophecies is about the awakening of the INNER Christ presence on a worldwide scale. That is what will bring an end to the present age of darkness on Earth and usher in "Thy kingdom come, they will be down on earth as it is in Heaven" – the Lord's Prayer fulfilled.

The last book in the Bible is called in Greek "The Apocalypse" or in English "The Revelation." Apocalypse means revelation in English. Unfortunately, the word apocalypse has often been misinterpreted to mean a cataclysmic destruction of planet earth. What this highly enigmatic book in the Bible is describing is the inner battle and transformation that takes place in each human when the inner Christ power awakens and then challenges all that is of the inner anti-Christ. "An Allegorical Understanding of REVELATION (KJV)" by Kelly-Marie Kerr can be found at: www.seekvision.co.uk It gives a detailed interpretation and commentary on the Bible Book of "The Revelation."

At the end of this age it is prophesied that such an awakening will occur on a massive, worldwide scale due to infusions of Divine Grace into the planet from the Central Spiritual Sun of God (see Appendix III of this book). Eastern and Western astrologers both "independently" indicate 2025 as the year when dramatic geological, social and political changes in the external world will become apparent due to the inner and outer effects of the manifestations of Divine Grace upon the Earth.

Those who Saint Paul called "the rulers of the darkness of this age (eon)" (Ephesians 6:12) have much to be concerned about by the global spiritual awakening. They sense it coming and will do everything with their negative power to distract and steer humanity away from the awakening of the inner Christ power. (Please read the Foreword of this book for an elaboration of the anti-Christ agendas.)

As we approach the end of this age there is a great opportunity for those who are ready to be transformed "in the twinkling of an eye." It will not be sufficient to engage in wishful or delusional thinking that this transformation can occur merely by believing that it has been prophesied and imagining that you will be one of the "chosen" or "elect" ones.

You have to choose to be "elected" by intentionally cultivating the Christ within through discipline, discernment, devotion, detachment, courage and purity of heart. The whole purpose of this book is to share the wisdom, guidance and inspiration to make the personal changes necessary to purify the false ego and become among those who Christ referred to when he said: "Blessed are the pure of heart for they shall see God" (Matthew 5:8 KJV).

Finally, in speaking about the second, planetary coming of the Christ within, Jesus is quoted in the Bible as saying: "But as the days of Noah were, so shall also the coming of the Son of man be." (Matthew 24:37, Luke 17:26, KJV) If you equate Son with Sun you will understand the mystical meaning of what Jesus said. (see Appendix III).

However, another meaning of the Noah reference has been revealed to me. Typically, it is thought that Jesus meant that there will be another worldwide catastrophe as in Noah's time that will then prepare the way for the physical return of Jesus. But again, let us consider also a different interpretation. Actually, it was Saint Augustine who wrote: "When you see numbers in Scripture, it would be wise to consider a mystical interpretation."

We are told in the story of Noah's ark and the Great Flood that Noah entered the ark in the second month and came to rest on the mountain on the 17th day of the 7th month. Those numbers are highly meaningful and not arbitrary or to be even taken literally. Saint Augustine would agree. From reading this book you should now be aware of the teachings regarding the seven chakras. They are numerous throughout the Bible – for example, the Menorah in the Book of Revelation.

Let us consider that the escape to safety above the turbulent, drowning waters of human existence occurs when there is an awakening of the Christ within that creates our own individual Light Body ark of salvation. Entering the ark in the second "month" is a reference to the second chakra. In the "five-element theory" that chakra is associated with "water." The second chakra is also related to the sexual organs. Thus, the journey of Noah's ascension above the waters of life begins at the second chakra and ends at the 7th crown chakra when the energy of sexuality is raised and creates a radiant "crown of glory that will not fade away" (James 1:12, 1 Peter 5:4, Rev 2:10).

CHAPTER **33**

How to Raise the Sacred Secretion

"If we honestly desire the good, noble things of life, we can live as we think and thus help to make a glorious heaven here on earth; a real, sincere, friendly brotherhood of men and women; free of greedy, selfish and immoral strife and ill will toward each other. Why not try for it? Truly, this is the eternal prayer of all upright men and women, to have peace and harmony here on earth."

(Page 43) [Mysteries of Sex] "The Light of Egypt" by Thomas H. Burgoyne

I have decided to break this chapter down under five sub-headings - all of equal importance. They are: Nutrition, Exercise (Specifically Yoga), Prayer (Talking to God), Meditation (Listening to God) and Attitude.

As mentioned in Chapter 29, the preservation of the Sacred Secretion involves offering our ten percent conscious mind to God for ten percent of the Luni-Solar month beginning from when the moon enters the void before entering your individual sun sign. This means giving our first fruits - our first attention, first love, first works, first gratitude, first acknowledgements, first faith etc. "Seek ye first the Kingdom of

God and his righteousness and all these things shall be added unto you." Matthew 6:33. Seeking "his righteousness" means sacrificing our carnal desires, thoughts and actions; over-eating, drinking alcohol, being prideful, being stingy, lustful etc. all of which will dilute and disempower the Sacred Secretion.

There have been many instances when I have been asked: "Do I have to fast?", "How many days am I not allowed to have sex for?" and "What is your exact routine to raise the Sacred Secretion?" etc. I am sorry to say it, but although this chapter will offer my personal insights for "getting close to God" and "raising the Sacred Secretion", for the most part these questions should not and cannot be answered by some kind of gimmicky "promised formula". So please don't allow anyone to tell you that they can. The reason being is that although these questions can all arise from sincere intentions, they may also conjure up the fateful issue of "giving to get, rather than giving to give." You see, all of the guidance offered here came from a genuine desire to know God, understand God and feel close to God continuously. Therefore, if you too are in that same place you should find the following ideas useful and effective. However, if you are merely looking to "raise the Sacred Secretion" you might not experience the desired results. You may still feel some results, but without a true heart for God (goodness, love, truth and peace) they will be limited.

"Blessed are the pure in heart: for they shall see God."
Matthew 5:8 (KJV)

With that said, I will now give a basic outline of my own, personal "routine" before entering into a more detailed guideline for each topic. Note, nothing in the following discussion or anywhere else in this book should be considered as a substitute for competent, licensed, professional medical or psychological advice, guidance or treatment.

Nutrition:

- I am a full-time Vegan, although I do allow myself the odd "day off" for social events such as a friend or family member's birthday where there will be cake!

- From the day of the void, before the moon enters my sun sign (see Chapter 30 for further details), and for the following 7 days I do the FULL Daniel fast. There are lots of really helpful books available to guide you on this subject but, generally speaking, this means a natural, plant-based diet with NO processed foods and NO caffeine. At other times during the month, I do allow myself to eat processed foods such as coconut milk, soya milk and vegan chocolate – but not on the Daniel fast, "Sacred Secretion" days.

- On these 7 days, I also try to leave a 16-hour gap between my last and first meal of the day in order to promote melatonin synthesis (see Chapter 5 for details). For example, if I have dinner at 6pm I will not eat breakfast until 10am. I do, however have infused water (more on this below) and caffeine-free teas during the daily 16-hour fast.

"The reduction of food intake increased melatonin levels in all tissues investigated, particularly in the stomach and the brain."

The Journal of Pineal Research [January 1992] "The effect of food deprivation on brain and gastrointestinal tissue levels of tryptophan, serotonin, 5-hydroxyindoleacetic acid, and melatonin" By G.A Bubenik, R.O Ball and S.F Pang

Exercise:

- Generally speaking, I am quite active - running around at the park and soft-play centres with my son, being a wife while balancing my work life with my social life. But I also make time for yoga.

- I have enjoyed doing yoga for many years now and, as will be disclosed in more detail later, I have gradually honed my practise to incorporate all of the different disciplines of the early Essene Christians.

- On the "Sacred Secretion" days I do my yoga first-thing in the morning.

Prayer:

- I pray full time, but you could say that my "formal" prayer time is during and after my yoga practise. I also pray when I put the kettle on in the morning, when I'm driving and whenever else there is an opportunity to talk to God - I pray, pray, pray. On the "Sacred Secretion" days I pray for specific things that I would like to understand, such as "please shine a light on the reason why I keep failing in a certain area" or "allow me to understand where the pain in my shoulders stems from."

Meditation:

- I always meditate immediately after I have completed a yoga practise - regardless of whether I have time to do 55 minutes, 35 minutes or just 5 minutes.

- On my "Sacred Secretion" days, I also meditate in my bed as I fall asleep (always sleep with a pen and paper next to your bed, some of your best insights will come at night or upon awakening in the morning).

- Some of you won't like this one, and I understand why, but I read the Bible a lot and meditate on its words. I do not do this because I regard myself as "religious" and nor do I wish to take a boundary-building stance against any other belief. I do not think that the Bible is the only "word" of God. I read it because the "Word" is GOD - which means more than you may first realise. The Word of God ignites hope, love, reason and delight within me which in turn draws hope, love, reason and delight to me. I set aside extra time in the early mornings on my "Sacred Secretion" days specially to read the Bible and other sacred texts.

Attitude:

- I just try my hardest to be loving and grateful as much as humanly possible. Obviously, there are times when we are "tested". However, remembering to go with the flow and surrender those carnal traits, such as ego and vengeance, will go a long, long way.

The final thing to mention before we look at each of these subjects more closely is sex. There is a LOT of debate about this particular topic. I get questions all the time such as "does it count if I have sex with someone that I love?" or "does it count if I orgasm but do not release the fluid?" My straight, honest answer is: I don't know. The arguments put forward by experts especially in the teachings of Kaya Kalpa are certainly compelling, but I personally prefer to completely abstain from sexual activity during the specific "Sacred Secretion" days.

Nutrition (Food and Water)

"The fruit of "the tree of life", or "the tree of good and evil" is good if saved and cast upon the waters (circulation to reach the Pineal gland; and evil if eaten or consumed in sexual expression, or by alcoholic drinks or gluttony that causes ferment – acid and even alcohol in the intestinal tract – thus no drunkard can inherit the Kingdom of Heaven, for acids and alcohol cut, or chemically split, the oil that unites with the mineral salts in the body and thus produces the monthly seed."

(Page 90) "God-Man: The Word Made Flesh" by George W. Carey and Ines Eudora Perry.

A HEALTHY body is incredibly efficient at keeping our PH levels normal (7.35-7.45) and it's at this normal level that our cells can function properly:

- Above 7.45 the body will be in metabolic alkalosis
- Below 7.35 the body will be in a state of metabolic acidosis.

The acidity and alkalinity of our food massively affects our vital organs, CSF and blood. It affects them by raising and lowering the body's natural PH levels.

The physical element of the Sacred Secretion follows the same path through our temple-bodies, "the temple of his body" (John 2:21 KJV) as our CSF, meaning that diet can and DOES affect spirituality and our personal relationship with our magnificent Creator. Symptoms of acidosis are: headaches, lethargy, weakness, fatigue, breathing difficulties, confusion and anxiety.

James 2:14 tells us that "faith without works is dead". Therefore, there is no point in praying and believing without putting in the work that is required to complement our faith. Part of this "work" is to honour our amazingly-crafted, God-made bodies and keep them functioning at their optimum capacity.

To maintain a balanced pH our bodies pull minerals, such as potassium, sodium, calcium and magnesium from its tissues in order to neutralize acid in the blood. Kidneys filter excess acid out of the body through urine, so you can imagine how hard the poor kidneys must have to work if our diets are extremely acidic. Although our bodies are brilliantly designed by God to regulate our PH, it is up to us to assist it by honouring our bodies with clean alkaline-producing foods.

PREVENTING PH IMBALANCE

Due to prominent levels of acidity in animal products our bodies will naturally be more balanced when following a vegan diet.

Genesis 1:30 explains how God intended for all living creatures to use plants for "meat":

> "to EVERY beast of the earth, and to EVERY fowl of the air, and to everything that creeps upon the earth, wherein there is life, I have given EVERY GREEN HERB FOR MEAT: and it was so."
>
> Genesis 1:30 (KJV)

Interestingly, etymology teaches us that the original word for meat, "mete", only meant "food", or "item of food". It wasn't until about 1300 that the meaning of the word "meat" was narrowed to be "flesh used for food". So, the word "meat" in the Bible does not necessarily mean "flesh" at all.

The "Daniel" fast is renowned as a way to honour God and complement our prayers. For the most part the Daniel fast incorporates the same guidelines as the "vegan" diet. Although, there were no processed meat and dairy alternatives in Daniels day – which is why the Daniel fast differs slightly to the commonly known vegan diet, as it allows no processed foods whatsoever. The "Daniel" fast kept the metaphorical lions at bay and brought Daniel closer to God.

> "God gave them knowledge and skill in all learn-
> ing and wisdom: and Daniel had understanding
> in ALL visions and dreams."
>
> **Daniel 1:17 (KJV)**

BODY-ALKALISING WATER (Infused Water)

Since the body is made up of 60-70% water, a wonderful way to assist the body in the preservation of the Sacred Secretion is by keeping our body's pH level neutral by drinking water that is infused with alkalising foods. Thus, making it more like the water that God originally created for us.

Untouched water in its natural state is high-alkaline (usually pH 9+) and is rich in minerals. God created the water like this for a reason - to restore and regenerate our bodies with oxygen and minerals. Since the water available through our taps and shops has been highly processed and distilled for purification, it is extremely difficult to access water with a pH of 9+. So, after a lot of reading and experimentation, I now use a combination of lemon, ginger, cinnamon and pink Himalayan salt in my water:

LEMON

- Lemon is a strong antioxidant and immune system booster
- Lemons are amniotic, producing alkaline by-products when metabolised, complementing your body's wonderful design.
- Purifying the kidneys with lemon helps to insure a consistent balance in the pH therefore preserving the Sacred Secretion.
- The scent of lemon releases pheromones and oxytocin helping spiritual health by promoting peace and love within ourselves.

CINNAMON

- Cinnamon improves the hormone Insulin's sensitivity.
- The insulin hormone secreted by the pancreas signals the cells to absorb sugar. This helps the body regain a normal pH, thus preserving the Sacred Secretion.
- The astrological properties of cinnamon show that it's of the fire element, the sun planet and the Leo zodiac - meaning spiritually that it promotes protection, success and strength.

GINGER

- Ginger stimulates the circulation.
- Ginger releases anger, resentment, envy and frustration via the adrenal glands in the Solar Plexus.
- Ginger promotes a strong circulatory system which is vital in preserving and raising the sacred secretion.

- Ginger clears the endocrine glands and helps your body to carry nutrients to the places that need healing the most.

PINK HIMALYAN SALT

Adding a pinch of Pink Himalayan salt to your water (if you can bear the flavour) will really assist in raising the Sacred Secretion and seeing God "Face to face at Peniel (Pineal)" Genesis 32:30. This is because, as a conductor salt has the ability to raise your bio-electrical frequency.

> "If you want to find the secrets of the universe, think in terms of energy, frequency and vibration."
>
> Nikola Tesla in "Vibe: Unlock the Energetic Frequencies of Limitless Health, Love & Success" By Robyn Openshaw

We are ethereal (abundant Spirit) beings surrounded by individual Torus Fields (bio electrical auras). Absolutely EVERYTHING is vibrational (Galilee meaning: rolling, turning, circuit, energy or vibration). As our vibration changes our bio-electrical frequency alters. If our vibration is of health and love then our bio-electrical frequency will rise and, as it says in Proverbs 3:8, "Your body will glow with health, your very bones will vibrate with life!"

Doctor Cousens calls Iodine, "Illumodine", and says it is the "Yod" in the Sacred name of God - "Yod Hey Vav Hey". Iodine or "Illumodine" makes ATP and energy. It is the activator of all vital bodily functions. A healthy Iodine balance in the body is essential for a favourable bio-electrical vibration and Himalayan Pink Salt (Organic where possible) is the easiest and cheapest way to maintain safe, God intended levels of Iodine within our human organisms. Just 1 gram of Himalayan Pink Salt can provide the body with 77 micrograms of iodine. Deficient iodine levels can wreak havoc on our bodies (including causing cancer development and growth). Simply put, Iodine is AMAZING but, be sure to do your own research as certain types of iodine are harmful. Iodine is found everywhere in the body it is: Anti-microbial, anti-bacterial, anti-mucus, anti-parasitic, a brain function supporter, anti-viral and an immune system booster. It also helps to decalcify the pineal gland.

> "Every vein and canal throughout the entire body, from youth to maturity, is being coated with carbonate of lime, or lime in some form (known as calcification). The coatings of the walls of the veins in such a manner, prevents the circulation of living matter; then, the real vitality of the food which we eat, is simply passed through the pores, or through the bowels, because it is unable to penetrate through the lime."
>
> Page 67 [Alchemy] "The Light of Egypt" by Thomas H. Burgoyne

Just as a showerhead or shower door can clearly be seen to become calcified by what we call "lime scale" from fluoride in water, the body and pineal gland can become calcified from acidosis and fluoride. The primary principle for living a long, healthy life is keeping all of the channels within the body free from the coatings of "lime". Clean alkalising foods (organic even more) assist in clarifying the body, which includes optimising Pineal function and subsequently Pituitary and Thalamic functions.

Top 10 foods for decalcification and a balanced pH:

1. Spinach
2. Lime

3. Kale

4. Avocados

5. Wheatgrass

6. Celery

7. Broccoli

8. Cucumber

9. Bell Peppers

10. Garlic

A great way to view the best sources of edible energy is by looking at the "Karmic Food Pyramid" in which foods are scored by their energetic composition and by physical levels of vitamins and minerals. By energetic composition I mean the emotions and karmic energies that cannot help but be attached to the foods by the law of nature; i.e. pain and cruelty.

> "Being a Vegan is not a diet. It is a conscious, responsible
> and ethical decision to make every reasonable effort to
> live and enjoy life without harming, enslaving, exploiting,
> depleting, contaminating and killing. It is the choice to
> be kind, compassionate and loving to all living beings
> on the Earth."
>
> Karrel Christopher www.vegansociety.com

For example, Chlorophyll is at the top of the Karmic Food Pyramid because, like sunlight, it is abundant to produce, regenerative in its composition and has a pH balancing effect on the body. At the bottom of the pyramid are things like processed meat because the animals have likely suffered great pain, not to mention the fact that, they have widely been injected with synthesised hormones which we would in turn ingest; acidifying and harming our bodies.

> "When the whole of this mighty scheme is taken into consideration, students will see how necessary it is for those who wish to develop their spiritual possibilities to live upon a purely vegetable diet, because the eating of flesh attracts the soul to the animal kingdom and degrades the higher senses."
>
> (Page 75) [Mediumship – Its Nature and Mysteries] "The Light of Egypt" by Thomas H Burgoyne

In the late 1800s Doctor Wilhelm Schuessler discovered that at a cellular level the human composition includes 12 salts (minerals). So quite literally we humans are the salt of the earth.

> "Ye are the salt of the earth: but if the salt have lost his savour, wherewith shall it be salted? It is thenceforth good for nothing, but to be cast out, and to be trodden under foot of men."
>
> **Matthew 5:13 (KJV)**

Just like the Scripture suggests, Doctor Schuessler theorized that many diseases and discomforts were caused by an imbalance or deficiency in these cell salts (minerals).

Each of the 12 cell salts is influenced by a different God-created astrological sign of the zodiac (to study more on this I recommend reading "Relation of the Mineral Salts of the Body to the Signs of the Zodiac" by

George W. Carey). The point I would like to make here in relation to the Sacred Secretion is that these salts are integral in establishing or healing the body at a cellular level. MRNA (Messenger RNA) cannot function at its optimal potential without a healthy balance of these minerals in its cellular environment.

The final point to raise in this section is about food quantities. The laws of nature mean that when we indulge in ANY food to excess the body will compensate by creating a surplus of sulphur and too much sulphur WILL not only have a negative effect on the physical expression of the Sacred Secretion within the Pineal and Pituitary Secretions but subsequently it will affect the Spiritual expression of the Sacred Secretion as well.

> "Fire and brimstone (the lake of fire) comes from the fact
> that sulphur (brimstone) is the prime factor in generating
> the rate of motion called, "heat" and over eating creates
> a surplus of sulphur."
>
> (Page 91) "God-Man: The Word Made" Flesh by George W. Carey
> and Ines Eudora Perry

Therefore, I would like to conclude this section by saying that when "seeking" to preserve the Sacred Secretion it is important to A) eat a no-processed-foods-vegan-diet (Daniel fast), and B) not to eat in excess (beyond the feeling of being "full"). At the very least, this should be from the time when the moon enters the void before entering your individual sun sign, to the time when the moon leaves your sun sign. Always do your own research, seek professional advice when altering your diet and please and take things one step at a time. If like I did, you have a few "vices" ask

God to help you quit them one by one. Commercial foods, drinks and drugs such as cigarettes and alcohol are highly addictive. It may take time to fully over come such addictions. Be kind and reassuring to yourself as you make gentle process and remember, every positive step counts.

Lastly, for those of you who have asked – I am sorry but cigarettes, marijuana and other recreational drugs (no matter how "natural") do of course alter our biological balance, hormone secretions and circulation and will therefore impede the preservation of the Sacred Secretion.

Exercise (Specifically Yoga)

It's a well-known fact that most types of exercise have a positive effect on the human body. Exercise increases strength, facilitates the metabolism and circulatory systems and in turn conditions the CSF and blood which, as we have been seen, are integral facilitators in Sacred Secretion preservation. Therefore, when honouring your body, it is important to make time for some form of physical exercise - whether it be dancing around the lounge whilst belting out your favourite (positively-themed) song, jogging, swimming, walking or doing gymnastics.

There is a lot of negative stigma attached to "Yoga" as a form of exercise, which we will be examining shortly. Suffice to say Yoga is particularly good for people with any level of fitness and works because it facilitates the flow of CSF and subtle energies through the body therefore enhancing the function of neuropeptides.

Neuropeptides are informational substances that are produced in the brain and fluid; primarily in CSF and also in the blood. These so-called "messenger molecules" distribute information throughout the body and coordinate the processes of life on a cellular level - including the transformation of melatonin and the production of pituitary secretions.

> "Yoga is the regulation and cessation of fluctuations and changes which are ordinarily expressive in the conditioned field of consciousness."
>
> Patanjali www.healtouch.com

With that said, let's debunk the lie that says Yoga is "demonic" or "false idol worship". Thanks to the writings of Roman author Pliny the Elder (AD 23–79), the Dead Sea Scrolls (particularly "The Essene Gospel of Peace"), the Nag Hammadi Library and Josephus Flavius Titus; a Holy sect of early "Christians" known as the "Essenes" can be studied in some depth. The Apocrypha of John describes the Essenes as "the immoveable race of perfect light humans". They are believed to originate from the time of Enoch ("7th generation from Adam" in Genesis) and just so happened to practice Yoga.

Yoga does NOT contradict Yahusha's (Jesus's) familiar teachings or inner, mystical teachings taught privately in secret with parables to his closest disciples. It precedes them. Research tells us that the Essene movement was started by Buddhist monks sent from India by the great Emperor Ashoka (whose name meant "he who regards everyone with affection") to Alexandria, Egypt around 250BC to work with Jewish, Egyptian, Persian and Iraqi mystics.

The scholars who translated the Dead Sea Scrolls, owned by the Essenes, found that the earliest forms of "Christianity" were based on the teachings of the Essenes. The Essenes were dedicated to perfecting their bodies and souls to become more angelic, in hope of restoring peace on Earth! The scrolls say that this teaching was given to the Essenes by otherworldly beings referred to as "the holy angels of the lord" or "the watcher angels".

Some of the Essenes lived in Qumran (home of the Dead Sea Scrolls) and it is believed that Jesus was one of them. We will use the name "Yahusha" instead of Jesus for this study because it appears 216 times in the first Bible (Torah) where "Yahushua" only appears twice, and of course, the English language name "Jesus Christ" doesn't appear at all (The Torah Institute).

The ancient manuscripts found at Qumran show that Yahusha taught the doctrine of certain prophets, for example; Jeremiah, Isaiah and Daniel. He also taught "The Essene Way" or "Essene Yoga". The Sanskrit word "Yoga" is a synonym of the Latin word "religion" which simply means "path to the unity or yoke with the Creator"; and it was this "path to mergence with the creator"; that is exactly the "Essene Way."

There are, however, many different branches of Yoga. So, which one was Yahusha teaching? The ancient Essene manuscripts reveal that "The Essene Way" was an amalgamation of several Yogic traditions including: Hatha, Bhakti, Jnana, Karma, Mantra, Laya and Raja. Each one assists an essential part of our spiritual union with God. However, to achieve unity with God in all aspects the combination of all seven practises is a potent blend.

Let's take a brief look at the yoga traditions included in Essene Yoga:

1. Hatha - Also expressed as/associated with "Asana and Pranayama" (the 3rd and 4th limbs of Yoga; movement and breathing).

The primary focus of Hatha Yoga is building control of the physical body – which in turn increases strength, resolve and determination of the mind. Movement does, of course, condition the body which is "the temple of the Holy Spirit" (1 Corinthians 6:19) and movement not only improves the circulation of blood, but also assists in blood purification - "the life of the body is in the blood" Leviticus 17:11.

2. Bhakti – often associated with Yama (outward conduct); the first
limb of Yoga.

Bhakti is a thankful disposition that expresses love for God. "The Essene
Way" teaches us to approach Yoga and life in a state of Bhakti, so that we
look for God's love in ALL things – in the "good" and the "bad". "Do not
be anxious about anything, but in every situation, by prayer and petition,
with thanksgiving, present your requests to God." Philippians 4:6 (NIV)

In my personal opinion, the disposition of Bhakti (unconditional
love), achievable through Divine Grace, is the most imperative foundation in the preservation of the Sacred Secretion because, the flow of
subtle energy within the body can be blocked by <u>any external force that
overcomes or shocks the body's internal ability to adapt to it.</u> The body's
natural capacity to adapt to physical, mental, emotional and chemical
external forces is determined by the individual's ability to accurately
perceive and adapt to day-to-day occurrences. Equally, the free flow of
mental impulses relating to CSF flow and electrolyte balance (the body's
electronic conductivity) in the central nervous system is vital.

3. Karma – The law of Karma is expressed in the Bible: "for whatsoever
a man sows, that shall he also reap." Galatians 6:7

Karma yoga isn't something that would be understood as Yoga in today's
world as it is not something that is necessarily done during a yoga practice session per se. It's serving God through love and actions towards the
world and others without thought of personal gain.

4. Jnana / Gyana - Also associated with Niyama (inner attitude) and Dhyana (inner inquiry) the 2nd and 7th limbs of Yoga, "His delight is in the law of the Lord, and in his law, he meditates day and night." Psalm 1:2 (NKJV)

Jnana also isn't what we now commonly perceive to be Yoga but has to do with knowledge. The knowledge that is obtained by asking ourselves questions such as, "What is my purpose?" and "Who is God?" To which we may find the answers in sacred holy texts or deep in meditation.

5. Mantra – "out of his mouth went a sharp two-edged sword:" Revelation 1:16 (NKJV)

The mouth is a means of expressing one's heart and the two-edged sword represents the two-fold power of denial and affirmation - one edge points to freedom and the other edge towards truth. Mantra Yoga uses the power of the spoken word (sword) and its powerful vibrations to manifest peace, light and love in ourselves and the world we live in.

6. Raja – associated with Dharana (inner concentration) and Samadhi (union with God), the 6th and 8th limbs of Yoga, "Be still and know that I am God," Psalm 46:10 (KJV).

Raja pertains to transcending mind beyond attachment to any carnal (matter-limited) understanding. It is silent meditation time that allows us to hear God's "still small voice" (1 Kings 19:12) and make space for God's vision in our lives.

Whilst practising Raja in a state of Bhakti, a total experience and understanding of the "I am that I am" can be achieved.

7. Laya – expressed as Pratyahara (inward withdrawal from the senses) or the 5th limb of Yoga and associated with Kundalini and Tantra

Laya Yoga is present in all traditions and pertains to the use of our breath. The Greek word for Spirit is "Pneuma" and it literally means breath and wind. Like Kundalini, Laya acknowledges the subtle energy of the Chakras and their coinciding physical glands. It focuses on raising the vibratory frequencies and energy (Spiritual element of the Sacred Secretion) within the body. In advanced lessons, Laya Yoga is also used to develop total authority over our senses.

Within the examination of these 7 yogic disciplines we can see that breath, movement, sound and meditation all work together to help physical, emotional, mental and spiritual blockages to dissolve. This sets us free from our attachments to the material world and deceptions of darkness thus giving God full reign in our lives.

Because Essene Yoga incorporates ALL of these integral spirit-nourishing yogic disciplines, instead of just one or two, it is arguably more powerful than any other form of Yoga.

FREEDOM YOGA

The completion of my research into the "Essene Way" or "Essene Yoga" lead me to create an App for iOS and Android devices called "Freedom Yoga". It incorporates all 7 aspects of this ancient Yogic tradition. There are both FREE and PRO versions available now at the App Store and Google Play Store.

"Freedom Yoga" includes:

- HATHA – building strength, coordination and flexibility in the body and mind.
- BHAKTI – using breath and prayer to invite and maintain a disposition of peace, gratitude and love.
- LAYA – Deep cleansing breaths in each pose and repetitive exercises with synchronised breathing help to stimulate the sacral pump and occiput thus charging Divine Energy, blood and CSF (the physical AND spiritual elements of the Sacred Secretion) up the spine.
- RAJA – Each practice ends with silent time.
- MANTRA – I have incorporated many powerful "I am" affirmations into each pose, thus remembering the power of Mantra given to us by our ancient ancestors.
- JNANA & KARMA – Scripture verses have been carefully chosen to complement the mood and vibration of each pose/exercise bringing knowledge and positive energy into the practice.

Here are the links to download FREEDOM YOGA on Android and iOS devices:

ANDROID – BASIC:
https://play.google.com/store/apps/details?id=com.seekvision_freedomyoga_basic

ANDROID – PRO:
https://play.google.com/store/apps/details?id=com.seekvision_freedomyoganew_pro

App store – BASIC:

https://itunes.apple.com/us/app/freedom-yoga-basic/
id1427558148?mt=8

App store - PRO:

https://itunes.apple.com/us/app/freedom-yoga-pro/id1427732315?mt=8

NOTE: There is also a FREE sample of FREEDOM YOGA available on my website at: https://www.seekvision.co.uk/freedom-yoga

THE VAGUS NERVE

This section would be incomplete without taking time to remind ourselves about the importance of the Vagus nerve. It is the longest cranial nerve in the body extending from the brain stem down through the body. It has roots within the abdomen, heart, oesophagus and the lungs - to name a few. It forms the autonomic or involuntary nervous system and therefore all of the subconscious actions of the body - a topic that will be discussed again in the meditation section of this chapter.

One of the reasons that the Vagus nerve is so vital in the preservation of the Sacred Secretion is that it is part of the parasympathetic and sympathetic nervous systems and its functions and health drive our wellness or disease. The body needs to be in parasympathetic, not sympathetic, dominance for healing and the all-important melatonin enhancement to take place.

The sympathetic nervous system is responsible for stress response and therefore has subconscious control over stress hormone secretions such as cortisol and epinephrine. These have a negative effect on the chemicals related to the preservation of the Sacred Secretion. For simplicity, I like to think of the sympathetic nervous system as the system that manifests our fearful emotions causing them to wreak havoc on the body.

Vagus nerve dysfunction (sympathetic nervous system dominance) can result in a whole host of problems including obesity, bradycardia (abnormally slow heartbeat), difficulty swallowing, gastrointestinal diseases, fainting, mood disorders, B12 deficiency, chronic inflammation and seizures. This can all occur because the basic, necessary bodily functions such as digestion, circulation and blood purification become restricted when we are fearful or stressed as the sympathetic nervous system has to automatically prioritize survival and recovery over them. Just like when we are trying to complete our work, but someone keeps interrupting us.

The parasympathetic nervous system optimises calmness, healing and bliss. It puts us in "rest and digest" mode and helps blood and CSF flow to the brain. Parasympathetic nervous system dominance supports creativity, reduces anxiety and produces clarity by allowing all of the body's systems to work in harmony with one another. Parasympathetic nervous system dominance can even improve the symptoms of conditions such as: heart disease, tinnitus, migraines, alcohol addiction, Alzheimer's and obesity to name a few! I like to think of the parasympathetic nervous system as an internal soulmate. One who comforts me and reminds me to limit my exposure as far as rationally possible to negative energies or react to low vibratory frequencies such as violent television shows, argumentative people, stressful situations etc. - thus keeping my "fearfully and wonderfully-made" body temple of the Holy Spirit in a vibrant and clear condition.

So how can we cultivate parasympathetic nervous system dominance? Let's look at a few easy suggestions. You may notice that some of these again correlate with the practices of the ancient race of "immoveable light beings" explained earlier:

1. Breathing Exercises – Simply pausing to take some long, slow, deep breaths will help. Better still, there are numerous books and articles on breathing techniques to study if you would like to get into it in more depth.

2. Showers and Baths - The sensation of water on the body relaxes us and therefore helps the body to switch into the parasympathetic mode.

3. Singing and Humming - The Vagus nerve is linked to the vocal cords. Therefore, singing or humming a sound or song that makes you feel good will raise your vibratory frequency.

4. Exercise - Growth hormones produced when exercising assist the vagus nerve and the brain's mitochondria thus helping to reverse cognitive decline. Yoga, in particular, increases the calming neurotransmitter Gamma Amino Butyric Acid (GABA) which facilitates parasympathetic nervous system dominance.

5. Massage – Massaging the feet and neck stimulate your vagus nerve. A neck massage can help reduce seizures. A foot massage help can lower your heart rate and blood pressure. An acupressure massage can also activate the vagus nerve.

6. Smiling – Controlled, scientific experiments have demonstrated that smiling stimulates the vagus nerve in a beneficial way. Smiling also has a positive effect on the vagus nerve of people nearby. A subtle smile can also be projected inwardly during meditation to open the heart and facilitate a spontaneous "relaxation response" in chronically, constricted areas. Thus, one can smile to feel happy and not just smile when we are already feeling happy.

Prayer (Talking to God)

"There is a trinity of laws to be observed; 1- Physical harmony and cleanliness in one's surroundings. 2- Mental peace and clean thoughts and freedom from worldly cares. 3 – Spiritual purity, and complete isolation from impure currents of thought. Evolve these states from within and the without will take care of itself. Honest desire (prayer) must be first."

[Chapter 15: Religion] "An Introduction to Sociology" by William Little

God needs us to be great "prayers"'. One of my favourite quotes is: "talking to God is prayer and listening to God is meditation." This is so true! God NEEDS us express our thoughts, frustrations and desires through talking and to take the time to listen for the answers. Both prayer and meditation are integral to the preservation of the Sacred Secretion. I always start my prayers by thanking God for all of my blessings big and small - both the blessings that I am conscious of and the blessings that I am not aware of. The emotion of gratitude resonates on an extremely powerful frequency and expressing it allows love, light and contentment to grow in your life exponentially - both internally and externally.

Our prayers should be passionate and strategic. They should not merely be "please God I need more money, more fame..." but predominately selfless. Such as, "please God touch the lives of those who don't know you, bring healing to those who are suffering and help me to be a beacon of Light in all aspects of my life that I may serve and honour your unconditional Love." Our prayers should be for the cloudiness and confusion in the world to disappear and the lies to be exposed on a mass scale.

God loves us and wants us to have the things that we enjoy. But try stopping for one moment and thinking about what you REALLY want… Is it really a new car that you want, or is it security? Perhaps the idea of a new car is attached to a deeper desire. Maybe there is a need to release the residue of negative energy left over from fearful experiences of poverty, lack, failure or people not taking you seriously? In which case the favoured and most effective prayer would not be, "please God give me a new car", but "please God release me from these feelings of insecurity and the spirit of lack". Because, when the stale, festering (d)evils in the shape of; past hurts, worries and disappointments get obliterated one by one that's when our clarity of vision becomes super powerful and our prayers really start getting answered.

What we really need to ask for in every prayer is the seed that is integral for the fruition of the prayer, or for God to show us and unblock the mental and emotional barriers that stop us from being able to receive God's abundant treasure. Try asking God for clarity in your desires i.e. "please show me what thoughts and behaviours are keeping me captive or stopping me from being able to generate income and teach me how to replace them with peace, love, joy and success-wielding thoughts and behaviours".

When the quality of our thoughts improves and the choice of language that we use enhances we become exceedingly powerful at recognising and seizing the many wonderful opportunities that God places in our midst. Thus, the answers to our prayers are often found in these little God-created moments of opportunity that we must appreciate and nurture. Sometimes there will be so many stepping stones on the voyage to getting what we desire, that the destination will not be in view. But in retrospect, after recognising each stone, one by one with alert vision and sophistication, you'll be able to look back and say: "wow, it's so obvious why I had to come this way".

> "When Solomon finished praying, a bolt of lightning out of heaven struck the Whole-Burnt-Offering and sacrifices and the Glory of God filled The Temple (his body). The Glory was so dense that the priests couldn't get in—God so filled The Temple that there was no room for the priests! When all Israel saw the fire fall from heaven and the Glory of God fill The Temple, they fell on their knees, bowed their heads, and worshiped, thanking God: Yes! God is good! His love never quits!"
>
> **2 Chronicles 7:1-3 (MSG)**

And remember, this Scripture is not only talking about a physical building, more importantly it is talking symbolically about our fearfully and wonderfully made bodies. The sacrifices are our carnal desires; sex, cigarettes, overeating etc. The burnt offerings are our servitude to God's unconditional love (Bhakti) and the priests symbolise the false doctrines embedded in our minds since childhood.

One prayer that has been extremely useful in my own life is the prayer of Jabez. It's extremely difficult to stay on the straight and narrow path of enlightenment when people around you are causing you pain. Insults, neglect, manipulation etc can be extremely hard to stomach when we know in our hearts how much we love God and desire God's Love to emanate throughout the world. That is why Jabez prayed this powerful prayer:

> "Oh, that you would bless me indeed, and enlarge
> my territory, that your hand would be with me,
> and that you would keep me from evil, that I
> may not cause pain"
>
> **1 Chronicles 4:10 (KJV)**

This is a seriously powerful request and I can guarantee you that God loves hearing this prayer. This prayer asks for God not only to bless us and comfort us by walking hand in hand with us, but most importantly it asks God to give us the capacity to resist the temptation of doing evil ourselves and therefore stops us from causing harm and assisting the spread of (d)evil.

One of the problems with someone hurting us is that the carnal instinct longs to issue some kind of revenge - whether it's the silent treatment, a sarcastic comment or something worse. I know for myself how strong this desire can be, especially when the pain that the other person has caused consumes us with hurt and anxiety. That is why Jabez's prayer is so poignant, so powerful and so necessary because it will send God's comfort and strength bounding into our hearts where it literally lifts us above the pain and onto the eagle's wings. Needless to say, any other reaction in these situations will of course send a negative ripple into the cosmos which, due to natural metaphysical law of action and reaction, cannot do anything except find its way back to us. The way to stop negative energy from spreading is to let God have it and God will extinguish it and replace it with love, hope and positivity. No ONE and no THING can do a better, fairer or more inspiring job of assigning karma than God's natural law, so never engage in taking this on as your own responsibility.

A note on prayers for healing: God has made it very clear to me that I ought to mention my own frustrations when it comes to unanswered prayers relating to healing. I have prayed for my Mum to be healed from M.S. countless times! I have prayed for psychological healing, physical healing, emotional healing… you name it, I have tried it. I've prayed alone, I have prayed in groups, people have laid hands on her and spoken tongues over her, but so far nothing has worked or at least not to the tangible extent that I have hoped for. It breaks my heart because I love her an incredible amount and am so grateful for everything that she has done for me, but I never lose faith. I will be talking about the laws of nature in more detail in the "Attitude" section of this chapter, but for now I will say that the "laws of nature" are the reason why people remain sick or injured in spite of our prayers and that although things may seem hopeless, all hope and light can NEVER be fully diminished and ALL prayers no matter how old or failed they appear to be, CAN STILL be answered. All it takes is one tiny shift.

I'll conclude this section by saying that it is good to make prayer fun! I like keeping a prayer journal and targeting people whose lives I know will benefit from God's blessings and then watching as marvellous changes and shifts occur. Praying for others really is extremely rewarding – especially when the prayers come into fruition.

Meditation (Listening to God)

"Meditate upon these things; give thyself wholly
to them; that thy profiting may appear to all"
1 Timothy 4 (KJV)

Biblically, those who took the time to hear God were blessed; Joshua, Isaac and Luke are among those who mention the worth of meditation and Mary was blessed because she sat still and listened. Stop asking God for results, if you're not prepared to take the time to hear the reply. Silence is truly a virtue. Through practising silent meditation it's much easier to hear the voice of God. You don't have to do anything fancy, just choose a focal point in your mind's eye, I like to use the word "love" or "light". Then begin to breathe slowly. If your mind starts to wander and you find yourself thinking about the thoughts of the day, simply bring it back to stillness by repeating "light" or "love" silently until the thoughts melt away. It will get easier and easier to remain focused and soon you'll become brilliant at creating peace and silence in your mind. I usually find that God starts talking or showing me images just as I manage to silence that last niggly bit of mental chatter.

Meditating on scriptures can also be extremely calming, enlightening and empowering. One of my favourites is 2 Timothy 1:7, "For God has not given me a spirit of fear, but of power, and of love and of a sound mind." You can try writing this down and reading it slowly over and over again - really letting the power and vibration of the words resonate and heal you from the inside out. You can even break it down into strengthening "I am" affirmations by declaring silently in your head: "I am powerful", "I am loved", "I am loving" and "I am clear and confidently-minded! THANK YOU, GOD". If you've never done an exercise like this before, you may wonder how it can possibly have a lasting, or life-altering effect. But like we discussed earlier; in Genesis it states that "In the beginning was the word and the word was God and the word IS God!" Do NOT underestimate the creative power dispersed into the universe in every word that you ever utter.

> "For there are three that bear record in heaven, the Father,
> the Word, and the Holy Ghost: and these three are one"
> 1 John 5:7 (KJV)

A lot of the wise guidance and direction toward the manifestation of our prayers can be heard or visualised during meditation. Be open to exploring the images that God places inside you while you are being still. Take a mental snap shot of them to use once you've completed your meditation and later you can reflect and ask God questions. For example, if you have a vision of three red balls ask, "what do 3 red balls mean?" Then, be open to noticing synchronicities and hearing divine guidance through dreams, friends, strangers, songs, TV shows, animal symbolism, number symbolism and the many over weird and wonderful ways that God finds to communicate with us. Believe-you-me, God will use any medium possible to get your attention! And God knows us all better than we know ourselves and LOVES to find ways to relate and create resonance within us and in our individual relationships.

There are many other ways to meditate and I encourage you to find a method that suits your personal preferences. Scientifically explained, meditation is a means of allowing the left and right brains to synchronise, hence moving brain waves into a slow and relaxed frequency. Day-to-day activities will usually keep our frequency in the beta brain wave region. Once the brain starts to synchronise, alpha waves, then theta waves and potentially even gamma waves will be produced.

> "As Marsha Keith has pointed out, modern neurological research has confirmed that meditation increases the levels of DHEAS and melatonin, secretions produced by the pineal and pituitary glands"
>
> (Page 492) "The Secret History of the World" By Jonathon Black

The slowing of the brain waves is what causes our consciousness to leave the analytical brain and move into the autonomic nervous system thereby accessing the subconscious operating system. The subconscious is responsible for all automatic body functions such as temperature control, digestion, heartbeat, blood circulation, plus; the aforementioned CSF pumps (namely the occiput and sacral pumps), and the all-important hormone secretions of the pituitary and pineal glands! The subconscious mind also regulates disease-fighting antibodies and blood sugar and has an important role in preserving the Sacred Secretion. The longer we can reside in a place of stillness and peace the more efficient the brain becomes at purifying, strengthening, regenerating and healing us - body, mind and spirit.

Scientific studies show that Melatonin levels in the body peak between 1am and 4am. Also, we know that it is the transformation of Melatonin into powerful chemical metabolites (see chapter 5 for scientific names), that are responsible for the lucid events associated with the preservation of the Sacred Secretion. Thus, the hours of peak Melatonin levels are arguably the most effective hours to meditate and or pray.

MEDITATION AND REMOVING BLOCKAGES

Let's look once more at the problem of "blockages" - one of the issues already highlighted within the "prayer" section of this chapter. Energetic blockages literally tie the body in knots. Holding on to a grudge or not allowing yourself to release pain through talking, praying and or crying will inevitably create energetic and physical blockages within you. This is why asking God to reveal your inner hurts and angers will be an incredible step toward allowing the free flow of spiritual Light and Love and physical secretions to transform your life.

> "I am the true vine, and my Father is the husband-
> man. Every branch in me that beareth not fruit he
> taketh away: and every branch that beareth fruit,
> he purgeth it, that it may bring forth more fruit."
> **John 15:1-2 (KJV)**

This Scripture explains how God removes everything within us that does not bear fruit (serve us) and "purges" or cleanses the parts of us that are fruitful. God does this to enable us to "bring forth more fruit" meaning that we can become more effective, productive and successful body, mind and spirit. The things that God takes away may be things that we think are helpful and are comfortable with but are actually standing in the way of progress on all levels.

Here's a simple way to practice releasing harmful energy in 4 steps:

1. Recognise the blockage

   The blockage will have been induced by some sort of self-depre-cating experience - either initiated by another person, an incident/set of incidents or our own self-limiting beliefs. If the blockages are not obvious to you or you don't think you have any, try asking God to shed a light on the root cause of your emotional and physical pains.

2. Process the experience

   Allow the negative thoughts and emotions to move through your system by letting yourself feel them and make friends with them (i.e. get to know them and figure out how/why they've controlled you for so long). Once you've examined the root you may feel the impulse to cry, forgive someone, forgive yourself or perhaps even rationally confront the pinpointed cause.

3. Transform the residual emotions

   Every time you find yourself dwelling on a self-limiting thought or negative residual emotion – STOP and transform that thought/emotion into a self-empowering one instead. For example, "why did he/she do that to me and hurt me so badly?" becomes, "everything happens for a reason, I appreciate the wisdom that I have gained through this betrayal". Or, a guilty feeling such as, "everything is my fault" can become, "I am strong, and I make wise decisions." You may find yourself needing to repeat this exercise over and over again in your day to day life. By God's power of cause and effect allowing positive, life affirming thoughts to become habitual will undoubtedly heal and transform your life for the better.

4. Bask in a positive thought or emotion

   Dwelling or revelling in an elevated thought or emotion during meditation is EXTREMELY powerful. For example, you could try mediating on the word "excitement" and all that it represents. You'll start to feel more energised, enthusiastic and happy within minutes thus immediately creating a wonderful ripple of love and fascination in the great infinite pool of life. Spending even one minute a day thinking, saying and daring to believe self-empowering thoughts like, "I am grateful", "I am joyful", "I am excited", "I am compassionate", "I am kind", "I am trustworthy" and "I am free" will change your life dramatically.

My favourite scriptural meditation and one that I've personally found the most effective is on John 3:30 (NIV) "He must become greater; I must become less." To me, pondering over this incredible scripture has brought me to the realisation that in order for God to fully use and develop our spirit nature, we must allow God's influence to show us the limitless power of Love in all situations. Through the revelations that God has shown me, by meditating on and praying this scripture, I've learnt that my human "perceptions" of situations rooted in thought and emotion will often be very limited and in some cases harmful to my health - body, mind and spirit. But, by allowing God to become greater and my "self" to become less, I liberate myself from limited, material, human perceptions and free myself to have unwavering faith in the abundance of God's unconditional Love to grow and penetrate into every aspect of my life.

To conclude this section in relation to the preservation of the Sacred Secretion it is important to remember how the body's vibratory frequency peaks and troughs in relation to our thoughts and emotions, subsequently having a direct effect on the secretions of the brain. Therefore, the more time we spend in a relaxed, positive mental state the more sufficient the body will be at raising and preserving the Sacred Secretion. Taking time to transmute or clear our stale low vibrational memories and past hurts will be invaluable on your journey.

Attitude (Seeking)

Having already discussed the disposition of "Bhakti" (loving devotion) within the "Exercise" section of this chapter, I won't go into it in detail here, but I would like to say that seeking to maintain an attitude of love in all aspects of life will go a long way toward preserving and raising the Sacred Secretion.

For the most part we perceive life via five senses, but this perception is not entirely true to reality. Quantum physics shows that even space and time are illusions. Ernest Rutherford performed an experiment in Manchester, England revealing the composition of the atom. Scientists were shocked to find that the atom is almost entirely empty space. Meaning that at an atomic level, EVERYTHING is connected. Understanding the common spiritual bond between all things in the universe and that we are all part of one Divine Intelligence means that nothing is unexplainable.

The perceptions that we have of our individuality and lives, such as our emotions, are just a small part of the true reality of a higher consciousness (John the Baptist). Emotions are a part of life that we cannot experience with our five senses, so how is it that we are aware of them at all? What most people think of as an emotion is not truly the emotion itself, but an experience caused by the physical manifestation of the emotion. For example, the emotion of anger causes disturbance in the psyche, thus causing the heart rate to increase and body temperature to rise – it is only then that we "feel" the physical manifestation via our "feelings" - making us able to distinguish and recognise it. Doctor Erika Rosenberg defines emotions as "acute, intense, and typically brief psychophysiological changes that result from a response to a meaningful situation in one's environment" (Page 225) "Synaptic Self".

Some Gnostics like to note the almost-anagram in "Amygdala": "Magdala" as in "Mary of Magdala". Emotive reactions activate the Amygdala which results in the automatic response of the networks that control a variety of instinctive behaviours such as: facial expression, freezing, fighting and fleeing. The autonomic nervous system (ANS) subsequently changes blood pressure, heart rate, hormonal responses (secretions) and peptides into the bloodstream according to the emotion. Simply put, when we experience emotions, they create signals in the body which return to the brain and cause physical changes.

Each "emotion" has a vibratory frequency that slots somewhere into the spectrum between the emotional extremes of love and fear. Fear has a long, slow vibratory frequency whereas love has a high, rapid vibratory frequency.

The long, slow fear-based vibrations are what inhibit us from activating the 64 possible codes of amino acids in our DNA structure made from five elements; carbon (Earth), oxygen (Air), hydrogen (Water), nitrogen (Fire) and phosphorus (ether).

Presently humans only have 20 active codes (20 amino acids) of the 64. This is due to the switches at the coding sites turning on and off in reaction to manifested emotions. This discovery was the first hard link between emotion and human genetics. Long, slow fearful frequencies will render the coding sites less active than high, rapid love-based frequencies which will have more potential sites for coding along the genetic pattern. Simply put, DNA alters itself depending on its environment.

It has been scientifically proven that photons (light particles) in the environment can interact with the DNA, causing it to reproduce what is known as phantom DNA. This may explain why the more we allow ourselves to experience an emotion, the more it will be perpetuated within the body. In other words, emotions directly affect DNA structure and replication and in turn shapes the physical experience of our everyday life.

So how can we begin to overcome fear and live consciously in a state that will perpetuate health and happiness in our lives? Reactive or animalistic (untamed) emotions are linked to the carnal mind and prevent us from reaching an enlightened state of consciousness and that is why "the carnal mind is enmity (opposition) against God" **Romans 8:7 (KJV).**

Let's look at how we can actively seek to overcome the carnal mind:

1. Be able to take advice or correction objectively without irrational defensiveness, resentment or rebellion. Do this by remaining peaceful and remembering that you are not in a hurry to reply to anyone - ever. Take the time to humbly ask God and yourself whether or not there is any truth in the other person's comments. Be honest with yourself and once a rational conclusion is found decide what kind and wise response (if any) to give that will manifest love and positivity in your life and in the lives of others. This does not mean that you should agree with everyone or let people bully you. You are entitled to be firm, be convicted in your choices and wear your "belt of truth". You may find it useful to simply say, "thank you for your opinion, however, I do not agree because… so let's agree to disagree."

2. Be able to accept neglect without hurt or insult. Do this by letting go of the need to refer to yourself during conversations or continually announce your successes or record your own good works. When you can truly love to work and do good for the benefit of others that is dying to self.

3. Be content. Do this by being grateful for every blessing big and small. Forgot what's missing and really relish in what you already have. You'll be surprised at how this matches your own vibratory frequency to that of abundance and thus opens the door for wonders and miracles.

4. Refuse to let anger rise in your heart. Do this by realising that humanity is greatly flawed and due to heavy, negative conditionings your good advice or opinions will often be ignored. Rules get bent and hearts tend to get broken. However, by not reacting with carnal reflexes all of these things can be endured with quiet, self-comforting reflection and loving wisdom. This in turn opening the door for signs and wonders.

5. Be free. Do this by soaring on the wings of eagles - floating above every base-level annoyance that has the potential to rob you of your peace and joy and inhibit you from exuding greatness into the magical cosmos where action and reaction is a certainty.

> "A current of love must descend so that the other one may rise to meet it at the source. Total force is born of this unceasing exchange and takes concrete form as a single fire, magnified that stands between the two: the fire of the Nameless One. Forever it remains the fruit of supreme initiation, the sceptre of Thoth of our brothers from the Red Land. Forever it remains the straight path of the true initiate who has made his way up the thirty-three rungs of the serpentine ladder."
>
> (Page 104) [The Labyrinth] "THE WAY OF THE ESSENES" by Anne and Daniel Meurois-Givaudan

A great way to understand how attitude affects us internally, as well as externally, is by reviewing the aforementioned Laws of Nature. Having mentioned a host of other guidelines and doctrines, it would be a shame not to include these laws briefly in this section.

Due to a lot of negative stigma, these laws are often overlooked or shied away from. But these Natural Laws are the fundamentals of science and predate Mosaic law or Biblical law. How can I say that so certainly? Because humans themselves predate Mosaic law - as does the universe. Even in the Garden of Eden, Adam and Eve had an innate sense of "right" and "wrong" long before the 10 commandments were recorded by Moses.

God gave us a conscience and compassion in order to feel and recognise the difference between right and wrong. Furthermore, since we depend upon God for absolutely everything, including the very air that we breathe for life, we should work to honour these true laws put in place to make the world a loving and peaceful place. God is Divine Energy. Divine energy not only makes but is also *in* the Laws of Nature.

Hermes Trismegistus was an Egyptian philosopher who authored the sacred texts that are the basis of Hermeticism. It is said that he received his knowledge while in deep meditative states. The seven principles of Hermeticism, also known as the seven laws of nature, are:

1. Mentalism
    The understanding that Universal Mind is infinite and that the "All" (True Reality) is this Mind and therefore, "Mind" is the master key.

2. Correspondence
    The understanding of Macrocosm (the whole) and microcosm (a

part); "As above so below" and "on earth as it in heaven." As in
a hologram, the image of the whole can be found in each of its
parts; each of us are made in the "image and likeness of God."

3. Vibration
   The understanding that nothing rests: EVERYTHING is moving
   - even the vibration of Spirit that appears to be at rest because it is
   vibrating at such a high frequency. Those who truly understand
   this principle can master their own vibration and reveal a wonderful Reality for themselves and others.

4. Polarity
   The understanding of duality: All relative truths are but half-truths.
   They have opposites and are not fundamentally different. For
   example, even black and white are just degrees of the same thing.
   Even hateful vibrations can be replaced by loving frequencies when
   we master the mind.

5. Rhythm
   The understanding that what rises will fall and that which goes
   out will come in. The pendulum will swing to and fro. The tides
   will always shift. To every action there is an equal and opposite
   reaction.

6. Cause and Effect
   The understanding that everything happens according to law,
   nothing ever entirely escapes nature's laws. Mastering the mind
   creates the ability to become a "causer" instead of being among the
   "affected" - a player instead of a tool.

7. Gender

   Everything has masculine and feminine aspects and together they manifest EVERYTHING.

Understanding and applying these principles can go a long way toward escaping victimhood and really becoming a catalyst for positive change and the development of unconditional love in your own world and the world around you.

There is also one other law, which although not commonly included in the list of natural laws is arguably the most empowering and progressive law of all. It is the Law of Forgiveness and Grace which Jesus demonstrated throughout his life on Earth. It was considered by many in his day to be a radical departure from the law of an "eye for and eye, and a tooth for a tooth" and has played a fundamental part in the progression of unconditional love and peace on earth.

8. Forgiveness and Grace

   The understanding that God Loves and forgives unconditionally and without limit. To master life is to acknowledge the law of cause and effect and thus operate from our Spiritual centre - the Sacred Heart. In doing so, we become instruments of God's Forgiveness and Grace as in the Peace Prayer of Saint Francis. Following the example set by the Sun, or indeed Jesus the "Son", means shining Forgiveness and Grace continuously - regardless of human behaviour: "for he maketh his sun to shine on the evil and on the good." Matthew 5:45 (KJV).

Thank you very much for reading this book. I pray that the information explored will bless you in the same way it has blessed me. I would like to conclude with this breath-taking quote as food for thought:

> "If only one-third of all the people on Earth came voluntarily, all at the same time, to send forth similar ideas of peace and unconditional love then the structure of all matter would be forever transformed."
>
> (Page 161) [The Land of the Red Earth] "The Way of the Essenes" By Anne and Daniel Meurois-Givaudan

APPENDIX

Exercises for Encouraging Sacred Secretion Preservation

In this section of the book I have included a few practical exercises that you might enjoy using on your journey with God.

1. The Prayer of the Energy Centres (chakras) by Kelly-Marie Kerr
2. The Breath of Life by John R Francis
3. The Radiant Heart by John R Francis

THE PRAYER OF THE 7 ENERGY CENTRES (CHAKRAS)
By Kelly-Marie Kerr

As discussed throughout this book there are 7 known energy centres (Chakras) in the human body linked to 7 integral glands and plexuses. The number 7 appears many times in the Bible reminding us of the power of this divine number.

Both the ancient understandings of the Chakras and the biblical references illustrate the importance of keeping each of the 7 energy centres clear to promote divine physical, mental and spiritual health.

> "The Holy Spirit manifests in humankind through these graces, reflecting the seven spirits of Yahweh. The seven graces are: 1) insight (prophecy); 2) helpfulness (service or ministry); 3) instruction (teaching); 4) encouragement; 5) generosity (giving); 6) guidance (leadership); and 7) compassion.
>
> **Romans 12:6-8 (MSG)**

Clearing and aligning the 7 Energy Centres (Chakras/Seals) is key when seeking God's divine healing, clarity and direction over our lives. Let's quickly recap on the role and importance of each energy centre and then follow with a guideline script for the prayer. The prayer script can be altered and personalised for your own needs. Make sure to take your time when praying this prayer, allow for the Spirit to move in you as you take your deep breaths and declare your affirmations.

THE 1st ENERGY CENTRE OR ROOT CHAKRA

Concerned with: Survival

Blocked By: Fear

When blocked it increases: Laziness, lethargy, loneliness, skepticism and anger.

When flowing it restores: Security, health, vitality.

HOW TO UNBLOCK THE 1st ENERGY CENTRE:

We must surrender ALL fear to God and let love lead.

THE 2nd ENERGY CENTRE OR SACRAL CHAKRA

Concerned with: Pleasure

Blocked by: Guilt

When blocked it increases: Feelings of guilt, possessiveness and shame.

When flowing it restores: grace, flexibility, depth of feelings, sexual and creative fulfilment.

HOW TO UNBLOCK THE 2nd ENERGY CENTRE:

We must forgive ourselves and surrender guilt to God and prayer for the ability to love as Christ does.

THE 3rd ENERGY CENTRE OR SOLAR PLEXUS

Concerned with: Will power

Blocked by: Shame

When blocked it creates: Self-doubt which can paralyze our ability to take action, assuming that we will fail, causing depression and confusion.

When flowing it restores: Motivation, enthusiasm, harmony and protection

HOW TO UNBLOCK THE 3rd ENERGY CENTRE:

We must accept that our disappointments are only part of our journey equipping us for victory.

THE 4th ENERGY CENTRE OR HEART CHAKRA

Concerned with: Love

Blocked by: Grief

When blocked it creates: obsessiveness, jealousy and bitterness

When flowing it restores: joy, gratitude and compassion

HOW TO UNBLOCK THE 4th ENERGY CENTRE:

We must lay all our grief out in front of us, let the tears flow and release the pain.

THE 5th ENERGY CENTRE OR THROAT CHAKRA

Concerned with: Truth

Blocked by: The lies that we tell ourselves and the deceptions that we choose to believe

When blocked it creates: an inability to express our self, defend our self and say no to things, ideas or people that don't align with our true nature

When flowing it restores: the ability to express our truth without worrying and the ability to diplomatically share our opinion with kindness, courage and conviction.

HOW TO UNBLOCK THE 5th ENERGY CENTRE:

We must ask God to show us our true power and who we really are, so that the lies and insults of ego and other human beings can dissolve.

THE 6th ENERGY CENTRE OR BROW CHAKRA

Concerned with: Insight

Blocked by: Illusion

When blocked it creates: moodiness, denial, irritability and distrust.

When flowing it restores: enthusiasm, the realization of our divinity and an innate sense of knowingness - all illusions will disappear.

HOW TO UNBLOCK THE 6th ENERGY CENTRE:

The biggest illusion on earth is that everything is separate – we are ALL connected. Even the elements are all one.

THE 7th ENERGY CENTRE OR CROWN CHAKRA

Concerned with: Thought

Blocked by: attachment to earthly "things" and "beliefs"

When blocked it creates: a fixation with people and things that have conditioned us to think within the borders of the visual human realm.

When flowing it restores: supernatural sight, visions from God and confidence in our own God given intuition.

HOW TO UNBLOCK THE 7th ENERGY CENTRE:

We must release ALL carnal thoughts, people and relationships to God, trusting that we will be eternally supported and comforted. LET THE ATTACHMENTS GO AND ENCOMPASS UNCONDITIONAL LOVE.

THE PRAYER
Dear God,

Thank you for the first spiritual energy centre of my body which becomes blocked by fear.

I know that you have not given me **"a spirit of fear, but of power, love and a sound mind" (2 Timothy 1:7).**

Therefore, I ask you to reveal all my fears to me so that I may fully release and surrender them to you making space in my life for health, vitality and security.

Let's affirm God's love over our fears:
Deep breath: I am safe
Deep breath: I am loved
Deep breath: I am secure

God, thank you for the 2nd spiritual energy centre which becomes blocked by guilt, today I ask that you forgive me for everything and anything that is hindering the free flow of total wellness and freedom in my mind, body and spirit. I am sorry for both the things that I am ashamed of and for the things that I may have done without awareness. I boldly declare that I forgive myself and that I am free to experience a life of joy, peace and success.

Let's affirm God's divine forgiveness over our wrongs:

Deep breath: I am free

Deep breath: I am forgiven

Deep breath: I am purified

Thank you for the 3rd spiritual energy centre which helps us to process shame. I pray that you strengthen and increase my faith so that I can powerfully step forward out of the paralyzing grips of past neglect, insults and disappointments. Please protect my heart **"like a wall of fire"** (**Zechariah 2:5**) and give me a wise spirit so that I can decisively remove all toxic relationships and habits from my life. I surrender all shame to you God and declare that I am healed in your holy name. Thank you for giving me authority over every debilitating thought and human exchange.

Let's affirm God's strength into our discouragements:

Deep breath: I am confident

Deep breath: I am enthusiastic

Deep breath: I am courageous

God, thank you for the 4th spiritual energy centre of love that becomes blocked by grief. I ask that you help me to courageously release all my grief by whatever means necessary and as the tears fall, I know that **"you are comforting me and healing me" (Revelation 21:4)**. I surrender all grief and bitterness to you and welcome spiritual waves of joy and hope.

Let's affirm God's sympathy into our pain:

Deep breath: I am healed

Deep breath: I am comforted

Deep breath: I am moving forward

Thank you for being **"the way, the truth and the life" (John 14:6)**. My 5th spiritual energy centre is in my throat and I ask that you fully restore its flow by giving me the confidence and wisdom that enables me to see, feel and speak total truth. Give me supernatural sight to discern any lies that are either being told or shown to me and all lies that my ego attempts to tell myself. Give me courage to be truthful at all times and show the power of who I really am whilst obliterating the insults and negative opinions of others from my mind, body and spirit.

Let's affirm God's truth over evil lies:
Deep breath: I am able to communicate my truth
Deep breath: I express who I am with confidence and kindness
Deep breath: I am a clear speaker and I deliver my words with grace and conviction

God, thank you for my 6th spiritual energy centre and has the tendency to become blocked by the illusion of separation. Lord reveal yourself to me in new and astonishing ways, be a constant reminder of the holy spirit coursing through my body and give me total assurance of your continuous and everlasting glory which empowers me to accomplish all things.

Let's affirm God's power within ourselves:
Deep breath: I am continually filled with the Holy Spirit
Deep breath: I am intuitive
Deep breath: I am a part of God

Finally, heavenly creator I thank you for my 7th spiritual energy centre at the crown of my head, I know that its free flow can become limited by attachments to things, people and beliefs. God, I boldly release all my carnal thoughts and desires to you, and I trust that I am totally supported and comforted by your unconditional love. Please help me to embody your goodness in everything that I say and do so that I can help to facilitate the end of all suffering and bring peace back to earth.

Deep breath: I am chosen
Deep breath: I am powerful
Deep breath: I am light

Thank you, God, for removing all limiting beliefs, toxic influences, debilitating lies, feelings of defeat, and all cloudiness and confusion from my mind, body and spirit.

Thank you for equipping me with wisdom, clarity, strength, confidence, power, peace and joy that I may move forward triumphantly; flowing with your endless love and limitless power.

AMEN

THE BREATH OF LIFE by John R Francis

> "And the Lord God formed man of the dust of the
> ground, and breathed into his nostrils the breath
> of life; and man became of living soul."
>
> **Genesis 2:7 (KJV)**

Those who know God intimately through direct, inner experience, feel God's loving presence to be in each and every breath. However, through conditioned disbelief or resistance not all humans live with a similar awareness. Faith in God's inner presence is a key to living with an awareness of God's Love. To have true faith is to trust God in our life – even for giving us each breath we need. Yet, our unconscious mistrust of God inhibits us from receiving our "daily bread" as the full life force in the air we breathe.

> "Man cannot exist without breathing, for the Breath of Life fills all spaces and is God in manifestation as Ether. This Ether or Prana Force is surcharged with Life-Giving energy and vitalizes into Living Life all external creation."
> (Page 3) "Scientific Rhythmic Solar Plexus Breathing" by Phoebe Marie Holmes

Breathing is the only major physiological process that is usually automatic but can also be controlled voluntarily – we can hold our breath. Mystics say the natural functioning of the body is not an entirely mechanical process. Rather, natural activity is sustained continually by the active, energizing vital-Love force of God. In other words, breathing can be a pure, natural expression of the loving Will of God in Creation or it can be, at least temporarily, overridden by the human will – we can hold our breath. This is just another example of the teaching that humans have been given free will by the Creator.

Holding one's breath can be life-saving. An example of this being, if one is suddenly thrown underwater or confronted with poisonous air. These are relatively rare circumstances. However, there are other ways which we hold our breaths unconsciously and continually - often due to the effects of emotional traumas that have not been fully healed. These effects have serious, usually unnoticed, consequences for the general health of body and mind.

When confronted with unexpected, emotionally-shocking events or news we usually unconsciously constrict our abdomen and hold our breath momentarily. This is described in common language as a "gut-wrenching experience." Furthermore, we might say when recovering from the shock, "I need to catch my breath." After the event there might also be a sigh of relief as muscular tension around the respiratory system is spontaneously released. In addition to this continuous sobbing may occur. However, after the initial shock has worn off there can be left some residual, unconscious partial holding of the breath that can persist unnoticed for years.

This chronic, unconscious holding of the breath manifests as constriction in the abdominal/solar plexus region and a resulting reduction in the air volume of natural, uninhibited breathing. Under such circumstances we are not fully using the lungs during breathing which naturally begins from the abdominal region via the diaphragm muscle. Breathing then is done more from the upper chest, is partial and thus unnatural. Therefore, less oxygen is being inhaled and less waste gases, such as carbon dioxide, and toxins are being exhaled. This can acidify the blood with the negative consequences previously discussed in this book.

Besides the physical effects, it is well known that the mind can be affected by incomplete respiration resulting in agitated thoughts and emotions. Anxiety, acute or chronic, can result from improper respiration - especially from an excess of carbon dioxide in the blood. Sudden acute anxiety, or even just irritability, for no apparent psychological reason might even signal an impending health crisis such as a heart attack.

Unconscious, defensive reactions to a stressful environment can also result in the continual, muscular constriction of the abdominal region and the resultant impairment of respiration. Toxic air, noise, electromagnetic and other radiations, crime, congestion, and negative or threatening interpersonal relationships can result in the unconscious, defensive physiological reaction called "armoring." This is referred to in the Bible as "hardening the heart" and having a "stiff neck." Psycho-physiological "armoring" manifests as chronic muscle tension and hardness. This "armor" prevents one from feeling or expressing Divine Love, Joy and Peace. Wilhelm Reich, M.D. did extensive research on "armoring" – a term he invented.

BREATH AWARENESS

The above discussion may seem speculative to some readers. However, if one sits or lays quietly in an alert, relaxed posture with steady attentive feeling of the muscular movements associated with breathing, discoveries can be made that will verify the assertions made in this article.

Breath observation may immediately reveal a sense of abdominal and or neck, face, jaw, chest, shoulders, arms, legs, hands, feet etc. tightness constricting and limiting full-free breathing. This may not be initially apparent but after only a few minutes of practicing breath awareness one may feel a spontaneous release of tension that had been constricting the breath. This is a form of chronic tension that the breath observer may not have even been aware of until it was released. This letting go can be accompanied by the proverbial "sigh of relief."

How simple awareness can result in spontaneous muscular relaxation is somewhat mysterious – even miraculous. The health and spiritual benefits are also far reaching. Since the chronic tension was unconscious perhaps conscious awareness acts as an antidote to trigger what Herbert Benson, M.D. has termed the "relaxation response" in his groundbreaking book by the same title.

The original word for spirit and breath is the same, hence why breath is also called "respiration" (which also has "spirit" as its root verb). Therefore, it is accurate to describe the Holy Spirit as the Holy Breath of God. A consequence of daily breath-awareness practice is a comforting feeling in the center of the chest. Thus, the Holy Spirit is named the "Comforter" in the Bible.

PRACTICING BREATH AWARENESS

A consistent, daily practice of breath awareness can have profoundly beneficial physical, emotional, mental and spiritual effects. Breath awareness is simple, yet it can be challenging.

An agitated brain-mind can have difficulty maintaining sustained focus on a single task. This is particularly true for attentiveness to an internal process of the body such as breathing. Normally attention is directed to the outer world and the brain-mind is engaged with those external perceptions. The brain-mind may also be thinking about past or future experiences in the outer world – worrying, planning, regretting, fantasizing, anticipating, calculating etc.

The brain-mind tends to be drawn outward and resists inward attention. The outer world seems so much more important and real than the inner. The outer demands continual attention since this is where we think all happiness comes from and also where all threats to our survival supposedly lurk. Yet, even greater happiness can be found within and equal if not greater threats to our survival can also exist inwardly. Thus, a seemingly wiser approach would be to balance our interest and attention in the inner and the outer.

BREATH-AWARENESS GUIDANCE

The typical unfamiliarity with the inner world makes an experienced guide for breath-awareness helpful. A guide should be one who has regularly practiced breath awareness over a considerable period of time. This guide should also be of high integrity and moral character and one who has a deep, inner and loving relationship with God.

A guide will be careful who he or she accepts for breath awareness guidance. For example, someone with a serious psychological diagnosis such as severe depression or psychosis should probably get permission from a therapist to proceed with a breath-awareness meditation practice. Also, certain medical conditions may call for prior consultation with a physician.

Furthermore, during breath awareness the relaxation of chronic muscular tensions may also release suppressed or repressed memories and feelings. A competent guide will instruct the breath awareness practitioner in how to release those surfacing energies and memories.

A guide may teach certain ways of facilitating the relaxation response such as tensing and relaxing of muscles or initial deep and full breaths. The projection of an inner smile into breathing might also be taught. Also, keys to breathing the feeling of Divine Love may be given.

The actual practice itself is effortless and simple but not always easy. It involves just being attentive to the full range of feelings associated with respiration and trusting God totally to do the breathing of the body. Trust is the essence of true faith. The whole body and soul are involved in full, holistic breathing.

Since fear is at the root of so much chronic muscular constriction the antidote of God's Love is essential. "Perfect love casteth out fear" (1 John 4:18 KJV). God's Love is always near. We just need to be open to feeling that Love with each breath. Repeating words with each breath can be helpful in opening to God's Love. "Yahuah" pronounced "Ya-who-wah" or "Yahusha" pronounced "Ya-who-sha" can be said beginning with the inhalation and ending on the exhalation.

> "Our souls become strong in spiritual power, for we are breathing the atmosphere of heaven, and realizing that God is at our right hand, that we shall not be moved. We are rising above the world, beholding Him who is the chief among ten thousand, the one altogether lovely, and by beholding we are to become changed into His image."
> "Selected Messages" [Book 1, 334.2] By Ellen G. White

Perfectly natural and healthy breathing occurs after the purification of the heart because only then is there no longer resistance to the breath of the Holy Spirit in the soul and body. We are encouraged in the Bible to not resist the Holy Spirit with a "hardened heart" or a "stiff neck" (Acts 7:51). The breath awareness meditation discussed above helps to soften a hardened heart and relax a stiff neck.

One of the consequences of purifying the heart through breath awareness meditation is that it allows the indwelling radiance of the Sun of God to shine forth. This enlightens the individual body and is a blessing to all receptive to this Divine Radiant Love. This Divine Light also provides needed guidance during a major spiritual awakening and throughout one's life.

It is essential to understand how important it is to center and begin ones spiritual practice in the Radiant Heart. It is known that the physical heart facilitates and regulates vital blood flow throughout the physical body. In a similar way, the Spiritual Heart, in the center of our being, regulates the influx of spiritual energies into the body and soul. This becomes extremely important when a major spiritual awakening occurs, and suddenly vast amounts of energy may flood body and soul. With this in mind one can now read the next Appendix: The Radiant Heart.

THE RADIANT HEART by John R Francis

This book has gone into detail regarding the physical and subtle anatomy of the human body and how it is designed to have communion with God. This exchange with the Creator gives access to the Realm of Heaven and all that it has to offer – peace, joy, love, abundance, healing, wisdom, creativity and more. This is why Jesus said: "But seek ye first the Kingdom of God, and his righteousness; and all things shall be added unto you" (Matthew 6:33 KJV) – all your desires will be fulfilled.

The radiance of the Spiritual Heart emanates Love, Light and Guidance from the central Divine Source of creation. It is therefore essential that the Radiant Heart always be at the center of one's spiritual practice and journey. It has the Divine Intelligence and Power to safely orchestrate the various changes in body and soul which occur during a spiritual transformation.

In this Appendix we will step back and look at the big picture to help the reader put into a cosmic context what has been put forward within this book. This will reinforce what has been explained and suggest new directions for exploration and understanding.

This book highlights the nourishment obtainable (body, mind and spirit) through the teachings of ancient yoga. In particular the chakras and the nadi system of the subtle body has been discussed. However, yoga also teaches about the multiple, encasing bodies that every human has. These body sheaths (physical, etheric, emotional, mental and memory) are called koshas in the Sanskrit of yoga. They are metaphorically referenced in the Book of Genesis when we read that God clothed Adam and Eve with "coats of skins." Mystics such as the early Christian Bishop Origen did not take this to mean that God literally killed and skinned animals to make clothes for the first humans. Rather these "coats of skins" where understood to refer to the physical and soul layers that cover a spiritual essence of our true nature. Jesus referred to these five layers in a parable as the "laborers in a field." Each of the five groups of laborers (layers) receive the inner light of the Central Sun in the reverse order they are encountered during the meditation journey to and from the Center.

Furthermore, yoga teaches that at the center of these sheaths is the True Self called the Atman. It can be first viewed mystically during meditation as a shining point of light – like a star. As we know, what appears in the sky as twinkling points of light are really very large suns similar to our own radiant sustainer of physical life at the center of our solar system. We might ask by analogy, when a point of light is seen in the center of our soul during meditation, what are we really experiencing? The mystics of many different spiritual and religious traditions who have gone deeply within during meditation have a common answer. That light point is the Central Sun of God seen from afar. It is not a physical Sun but a purely spiritual, eternal and perfect manifestation of the ground of eternal consciousness that underlies and supports all of creation. Metaphorically, this mystical star in the "manger of the heart" has been referred to as the "Star of Bethlehem." Its appearance in meditation heralds the birth of Christ Consciousness in the Sacred Heart.

Mystics tell us that this inner "star" is like a seed – a "star seed." When this seed "sprouts" it becomes a blazing sun that can light the whole world. We no longer feel ourselves to be just a physical body but instead a literal "Sun of God." Jesus actually told his disciples I have said, "Ye are gods; and all of you are children of the most High." (Psalm 82:6 KJV). The life of Jesus was a metaphorical demonstration of the path leading to becoming a Sun of God. If there is only one Central Sun of God how can any individual human also be considered to be a Sun of God? The modern physics of the hologram tells gives us an analogy by which to understand the process. It affirms the word of God in the Biblical Book of Genesis that states we are made in the "image and likeness of God." If we look at any tiny part of a holographic image of a Sun, we will see according to physics a replica of whole image contained in each part of the whole.

This gives us an idea of the purpose for being born on Earth and enduring all the hardships that human life involves. The negative challenges of life are opportunities to respond (and not react) in a positive way from our individual Sacred Heart seed. The positive neutralizes the negative and the spiritual star seed grows. That is the wisdom of the saying: "It is better to light a candle than to curse the darkness."

The following meditation offers a way to cultivate a positive response to life and become individual Suns of God for the benefit of all humanity and all living beings on Earth. All forms of life are essentially rays of the Central Sun of God evolving into multiple Suns of God.

GUIDED RADIANT HEART MEDITATION
Heart-centered meditation reveals true "enlightenment" as described by the words of Jesus: "if thine eye be single thy whole body shall be full of light." The "single eye" is at the center of the Spiritual Heart. From

that point of view oneness is experienced and transformation occurs by the Divine Light that radiates forth from that point. Meister Eckhart described it this way: "The eye with which I see God is the same eye by which God sees me." However, referring to brain-centered double (dualistic) vision, Jesus also said "if thine eye be double then great is the darkness" that fills a person's being. This gives a metaphysical meaning to what optometrists call "double vision." Metaphysically it means seeing life fundamentally composed of good and evil instead of as an expression of one-universal loving consciousness.

So now let us explore briefly how the shift from being brain-centered to being heart-centered can occur. Note: you will not lose your brain or mind. Rather, your brain will become an instrument and servant of your Spiritual Heart and thus your true Self. Also, in your Spiritual Heart you will be centered in peace and stillness as in the "eye of a storm."

Meditation should be learned directly from an experienced and ethical meditator and not from the printed word. If one suffers from depression, psychosis or other mental disorders a trained mental-health professional should be consulted first. Also, be aware that meditation has physiological effects on the body. According to Taoist yoga, focusing attention above the level of the heart, such as at the "third eye", may increase blood pressure. Conversely, meditation below heart level, such as on the soles of the feet, may decrease blood pressure. Radiant Heart-Centered meditation can restore blood pressure to a healthy normal as well as safely regulate influxes of higher levels of energy.

THE FOLLOWING DESCRIPTION IS NOT MEANT AS A SUBSTITUTE FOR PERSONAL INSTRUCTION.

Heart-centered meditation involves directing attention toward the deep center of "being". Relaxing the abdominal-solar plexus is a helpful starting place before going deeper. Projecting a subtle smile inwardly can also release constriction. The Cosmic Breath should be allowed to express and not be constricted. Attention can shift to the feeling of whole-body breathing and any Divine Love, Joy or Peace felt radiating outward from the center of the chest. Brain-generated thoughts are ignored as we gently return to the feeling mode when brain-thoughts arise. Heart-centering will then occur naturally and spontaneously.

Heart-centering is the effect of heart-centered meditation. Body and mind are inspired from the Divine Center and not pushed and pulled by external events. This facilitates resilience in the midst of life's challenges. We remain at peace amid external turmoil. We also radiate that peace into the world. Being in touch with the Cosmic Center we receive creative solutions to life's challenges directly from the Divine Source.

We also learn to distinguish between Divinely-inspired thoughts that radiate from the inner Sacred Center and those that are generated by the brain. Thus, we tend not to get caught up in brain-worry loops arising from the inherent fear-based "negativity bias" of the brain. But if we do, we know how to shift away from worry and back to a heart-centered feeling of radiant love. "Perfect Love casts out fear."

Sources and Bibliography

BIBLES:

"The King James Bible Version (KJV)"

"The Besorah Of Yahusha Natsarim Bible Version (BYNV)"

"The New International Bible Version (NIV)"

"The Message Bible Version (MSG)"

BOOKS (Alphabetised by surname):

"The Chemistry of Consciousness" Doctor Barker and Doctor Borjigin

"The Secret History of The World" Jonathan Black

"The Secret Doctrine" Vol 1. Madame Helena P. Blavatsky

"Isis Unveiled: The Secret of The Ancient Wisdom Tradition" Madame P. Blavatsky

"The Essene Gospel of Peace: Book 1 – Gospel of Peace" Edmund Bordeaux Szekely

"The Essene Gospel of Peace: Book 2 - The Unknown Books of the Essenes" Edmund Bordeaux Szekely

"The Essene Gospel of Peace: Book 3 - Lost Scrolls of the Essene Brotherhood" Edmund Bordeaux Szekely

"The Essene Gospel of Peace: Book 4 - The Teachings of the Elect" Edmund Bordeaux Szekely

"The Kundalini Process" Wim Borsboom

"The Light of Egypt" Thomas H. Burgoyne

"The Science of The Soul and The Stars" Thomas H. Burgoyne

"God-Man: The Word Made Flesh" George W. Carey and Ines Eudora Perry

"Relation of The Mineral Salts of The Body to the Signs of The Zodiac" George W. Carey

"Eternal Drama of Souls, Matter and God" Jagdish Chander

"Dark Retreat" Mantak Chia

"Philosophical Transactions of the Royal Society of London, Series B, Biological Sciences" Francis Crick and Christof Koch

"Becoming Supernatural" Joe Dispenza

"Monism or Advaitism?" Manilal Nabhubhai Dvivedi

"Nitrogeno 03: Making Gold" Autumn 2016, Fontana Editore

"The Secret Initiation of Jesus at Qumran: The Essene Mysteries of John the Baptist" Robert Feather

"The Twelve Powers of Man" John Fillmore

"Metaphysical Bible Dictionary" Charles Fillmore

"Talks on Truth" Charles Fillmore

"The Mystic Way of Radiant Love" John R Francis

"Palaces of God" Clark J. Forcey and Herbert Lockyer

"The World's Sixteen Crucified Saviours: Christianity Before Christ" Kersey Graves

"God, The Bible, The Planets and Your Body" Kedar Griffo

"The Occult Anatomy of Man" Manly P. Hall

"Think and Grow Rich" Napoleon Hill

"Scientific Rhythmic Solar Plexus Breathing" Phoebe Marie Holmes

"Light on Yoga" B.K.S. Iyengar

"The Biology of Kundalini" Justin Kerr

"Nineteenth Century Origins of Neuroscientific Concepts" Julien Jean César Legallois

"The Gospel of Thomas: The Gnostic Wisdom of Jesus" Jean-Yves Leloup

"The Gospel of Philip: Jesus, Mary Magdalene, and the Gnosis of Sacred Union" Jean-Yves Leloup

"An Introduction to Sociology" William Little

"Hypnagogia: The Unique State of Consciousness Between Wakefulness and Sleep" Andreas Mavromatis

"The Way of The Essenes: Christ's Hidden Life Remembered" Anne and Daniel Meurois-Givaudan

"Vibe: Unlock the Energetic Frequencies of Limitless Health, Love & Success" Robyn Openshaw

"The Living Message" Eugene H. Peterson

"Physiology Secrets" Hershel Raff

"Endogenous Light Nexus Theory of Consciousness" Karl Simanonok

"The Hope of God's Light" President Dieter F. Uchtdorf

"The Essenes, the Scrolls, and the Dead Sea" Joan E. Taylor

"Kaya Kalpa: The Ancient Art of Rejuvenation" Doctor Chandrasekhar Thakkur

"Secrets of The Body" Chris Van Tulleken, Xand Van Tulleken and Andrew Cohen

"Healthful Living" Ellen G. White

"Selected Messages" Ellen G. White

"Fossilised Customs" Lew White

ONLINE SOURCES (In order of appearance):

The Metaphysical Dictionary at www.truthunity.com

www.ncbi.nlm.nih.gov

www.Luminescentlabs.org

Strong's concordance at www.biblehub.com

www.Philaletheians.co.uk

www.collinsdictionary.com

[Video] "Meninges of the Brain" by Ken Hub.

www.neuroquantology.com

www.researchgate.net

www.vegansociety.com